Own Your Sh*t

Own Your Sh*t

HOW TO KNOW YOUR WORTH AND WHAT
YOU WANT—AND LET GO OF THE REST

James Boileau

Own Your Sh*t

For information, contact PO BOX 19112 Fourth Avenue Vancouver, British Columbia Canada V6K 4R8

FIRST EDITION

Designed by Amanda Fetterly and Sarah Reid.

Printed in Canada.

Library and Archives Canada Cataloguing in Publication

Boileau, James, author
Own Your Sh*t : how to know your worth and what you
want—and let go of the rest / James Boileau.

1. Self-esteem. 2. Self-actualization (Psychology).
I. Title. II. Title: Own Your Shit.

BF697.5.S46B65 2014   158.1   C2014-903112-2

ISBN 978-0-9937795-0-3

www.ownyourshit.com

To my mom and dad, thank you.

We Give a Sh*t

It is only when you *own* your sh*t that you can truly *give* a sh*t.

We at OYS give a sh*t about sustainability, education, and social enterprise. That's why we print responsibly and give $1 from every book sold to organizations that further education or social enterprise around the world.

Our Footprint

Own Your Sh*t saves the following resources per thousand books printed, by printing on 100% FSC post consumer waste paper.

ENVIROMENTAL SAVINGS

5	trees
4,920	gallons of water
503	lbs of waste
1,651	lbs of CO_2
4	MBTU
2	lbs of NOx

Environmental impact estimates were made using the Environmental Paper Network Paper Calculator Version 3.2. For more information visit www.papercalculator.org.

Contents

19   PREFACE

27   INTRODUCTION: **What is "Owning Your Sh*t"?**

PART I: **The Foundation**
35   Embracing Change
39   Putting Yourself First
43   Being Authentic
45   Listening Actively
51   Settling into Yourself
55   Asking Better Questions to Get Better Answers

PART II: **The Key Questions**
61   What Positive Did I Learn?
65   Am I as Overwhelmed as I Think I Am?
67   What Is Mirroring Back to Me?
69   Have I Really Grown Up Yet?
73   Where Are My Boundaries?
77   Where's My Focus?

79   Am I Actively Designing My Life?

81   How Do I Know When to Make the "Last Call"?

83   How Do I "Manage the Gap"?

87   How Do I Handle Judgment?

91   Am I Doing Too Much?

93   How Do I Define Success?

     PART III: **The Four Stages**

97   The Four Stages of Making Sh*t Happen

103   Stage One: Awareness

115   Stage Two: Choice

125   Stage Three: Action

145   Stage Four: Commitment

153   READY, SET . . . OWN YOUR SH*T!

PREFACE

The hardest thing I have ever done is write these words that you have in front of you now. I am not a writer, or even a good speller. I don't even enjoy reading that often. In many ways I am a very unlikely person to have written a book, yet here it exists.

This book contains the best lessons I've learned about life. I thought it should start with the story of writing this book, because we each struggle with a burning desire to create something amazing. This struggle causes us to ask a lot of universal questions and experience a lot of universal feelings, such as doubt and isolation. It can be downright torture some days, and euphoria others. My wish is that at least pieces of this book will inspire you to keep forging ahead on your journey and help you feel more connected to both yourself and to the people around you. I look forward to the amazing things you will do with your life. I hope they fulfill you and make the world we live in a better place.

What these words and ideas represent is not so much a book, but the ability and commitment to achieve something I wanted deeply. It is a fool's dream to simply want something and expect it to manifest itself without any effort. If you really want something, you must take consistent daily action to make it happen, and you must be more committed than you ever thought possible. You must value and crave your desired outcome at a level that stirs your soul and gets you off your ass. You must be resilient and persistent in your quest. You must embrace getting knocked down and be determined enough to keep finding ways to get back up. You must resolve to endure massive highs and extreme lows, and be capable of standing in the flames without setting yourself on fire. You must keep moving forward every day, even when the voice in your head screams out "mercy!" and everyone and everything around you says no, says you can't, and you feel lost and disconnected. You may look and feel like a fool many times along the way, but the real fool is the person who gives up early and never realizes his or her dream.

If I have learned anything, it is that human beings are capable of spectacular things. Look around you: We have created so many amazing structures, systems, and technologies from nothing but ideas and hard work. I believe we can have anything in this world, just not everything. It is in the choosing of what we want to create with our lives that we get overwhelmed, frustrated, and often paralyzed. But by understanding and putting aside many empty, distracting wants and interests, I have been able to focus on and pursue the passions and desires I know at a deep level are right for me. With some effort, attention, and the tools I provide in this book, you can do the same.

I started this book over five years ago. I knew that as a person who hated writing—and I do mean hated writing—the goal of writing a book seemed ridiculous. But I focused on the process and had faith that I would get to the end result if I followed it. My experience in marketing, entrepreneurship, and business, coupled with my unique new-age style of upbringing, told me I didn't have to be a writer to write a book. I just needed to be inspired by an idea and find a process that would work for me.

I always thought of my upbringing as disadvantaged. When I got into my midtwenties, I realized that the way I grew up actually set a unique and strong foundation that I now deeply appreciate and use to connect with and help others. I grew up differently than most people in the '80s and early '90s. For the first eight years of my life I lived off the grid. My parents were both from a major city but decided they wanted to live in remote Northern Canada instead. They purchased five acres of land and built a log house by hand. They grew their own food and worked only when we needed money for things to survive or play with, such as a snowmobile, gas generator, or a cement mixer. We didn't have indoor plumbing or electricity. The nearest town was a four-hour drive away on a dirt road. The landscape was breathtaking, and the handful of people in the area were hippies, loggers, draft dodgers, and trappers. I still recall not being allowed to play outside unsupervised one summer because there was a grizzly bear on the loose breaking into cabins looking for food.

It was here that I learned the simple truths of people and life. My incredibly bright, adventurous, abstract-thinking parents were brave enough to do things differently. They helped me build a healthy sense of self, of community, and of people in general. My parents exposed me to veganism, meditation, cleanses, astrology, holistic health, quantum physics, spirituality, and psychology. Despite the remoteness of our home, my parents were among the first people to adopt new technology like personal computers, satellite television, VCRs, and the Internet. After nearly a decade in the bush, we moved to the nearest small town. I lived there until I was seventeen, when I moved to Vancouver, Canada, and adopted the urban living I had begun craving.

My upbringing gave me the freedom and encouragement to openly explore and figure out the various boundaries of life and human behavior. Combine this with the ability to think and speak quickly, and I was a perfect recipe for adolescent trouble. It was in grade school that I really began to play with the rougher, more mean-spirited parts of life and teased people because it entertained me and won attention. I was always so good at it because I could see a person's weak spot—whatever he or she was trying so hard to hide or play down. It would pop out at me like a bright light, and I would poke that spot verbally until I got a reaction. Once I had a reaction, I was satisfied and moved on to my next target.

It wasn't until my midtwenties that I fully understood the mean-spirited nature of my teasing and put a stop to it. I learned that a great weakness could become a great strength. I realized that my ability to see people's patterns could be used to help them, and that I wanted to use this skill for something more than getting attention and a laugh. I saw my peers struggling with life and looking for answers, because the answers that school, our parents, and pop culture gave us weren't working out the way we were told they would. I was also struggling to figure out who I was, what I wanted, and how to understand this crazy world I thought I knew. My peers and I were becoming increasingly frustrated and jaded. By this point in our lives we had moved out of our houses, traveled, partied, got our degrees, and were starting to work. We were experimenting with dating and figuring out how to keep up with the skyrocketing cost of life and all the stuff we wanted. Most months, our paychecks didn't match our expenses. We wanted to buy condos, new cars, a couple vacations a year, and new clothes every season; visit all the trendy places we saw others going; and of course figure out how to pay down our massive pile of education debt. We were told we could have it all, but in the real world there weren't syllabi and scoring systems for passing and failing. We were on our own and getting increasingly lost and frustrated the further we pressed into adulthood.

My twenty-five-year-old self was compelled to figure this out and alleviate its own struggles. I recognized that the problem had to do with my own expectations and understandings. I could see that the beliefs, values, and experiences I was raised with were far closer to what I was looking for than what I had learned in school or through shiny pop culture. With this in mind, I dove again into self-help, communications, business, meditation, cleanses, astrology, holistic health, quantum physics, spirituality, and psychology. It was familiar and made more sense now that I was an adult and had a broader perspective on life. I saw common patterns and truths and began applying them to my life. Small changes started making big differences. I knew there was something there that was working for me and could also help my peers struggling with similar challenges. I needed to find a way to understand and synthesize all my changes, perceptions, and ideas, and create a simple solution that connected the dots in a way that made sense.

I started with myself. My goal was to get comfortable with who I was and to own my sh*t. The further I worked through this and the more comfortable I got with me, the more I was compelled to help my peers. There were lots of great ideas out there, but none of them were tailored to the specific challenges we were facing. I wanted to bridge this gap with simple tools designed to take the best of what existed, coupled with my experiences and expertise. Turning all of it into a book seemed like the best way to share these ideas and experiences, but I hated writing and had no idea how to write a book. It was going to take too long and be too much work. I tried to find shortcuts and ways to glamorize it, but every attempt I made to avoid the path of least resistance (the book) didn't work.

In the beginning, I struggled to write and clearly communicate the ideas I had in a manner that would be easily understood. I had no problem talking about them, but they didn't want to go down on paper the same way they came out of my mouth. The more I wrote, the harder it became. Once I had been working at it for a while, I was even more inspired by the idea but further challenged by the process. I didn't just want to write a book—I wanted to create an idea that both captured and shifted the paradigm of my generation. I knew this was a big opportunity; I just wasn't sure how to seize it. But I was committed and driven to find a way to make it happen.

Enter the most challenging five years of my life.

Writing this book was pure torture—emotionally, and at times physically. When I look back now, I don't remember each specific detail of the days, weeks, and sometimes months I couldn't write, hated all my ideas, wanted to give up, or questioned my commitment and myself. What I do remember is the persistent struggle and frustration. Writing and living this book was an enormous challenge. When the book struggled, it was because I was struggling, and the only way to finish it was to further own my sh*t. Each idea, chapter, and draft had to be fully understood and lived by me before I could put it in the book in a way that made sense. This forced me to constantly step up and make changes and face challenges in myself. The journey between where I was and where I wanted to go was exhausting. Knowing what I needed to do and actually doing it were two very different things. I learned that the process of writing this book could only go as fast as my own life's process.

Most of us have felt this emotional and physical challenge in our lives while trying to create something we really wanted. It's hard, but I promise you that if you truly want something, then going all in is the only answer. Throughout the process you must find a way to enjoy and grow and learn. I gave up a lot of things in the last five years to create this book. I could have taken a lot of different paths and my life would be in a very different place, but my choices have led me here. What you're holding in your hands now is the accumulation of all the times I wanted to quit but kept going.

The last five years were about getting comfortable with me. I consciously explored how I spent my time and what I thought about, and I examined what I knew to be true for me, what I wanted in life, and how I would go about turning those personal truths and desires into realities and lessons. Through this I found that at the basis of everything I stand for and believe in are two values: authenticity and vulnerability. I hold these values closer than anything else in my life. I handed out an earlier draft of this book to a dozen people for feedback. I kept hearing the same response echoed from the readers: The book had amazing content but my personality hadn't yet shone through. They reminded me that I was an edgy, in-your-face person who cared deeply for people, and that the book was missing the edge that they get with me in real life. But that edge was hard for me to write in a format that will live on forever and be open to interpretation and judgment by people who don't know me or don't have the context to fully understand me. I knew I would be judged, and who the hell wants that?

Putting my real self out here for the world to judge is scary. It is also liberating. When I stopped judging myself and no longer gave a shit about what might happen, I was able to do exactly what I wanted and feel proud of it. I knew five years ago when I wrote my first version of this book what I needed to do, but it has taken me this long to come to terms with it. I had to fully embrace myself and own my sh*t before I could put it out there for others. What follows is the end result of that hard work and personal journey. I hope it inspires and helps you along your journey—even if only in a small way. I know whatever occurs from here will be what it will be, and I believe it will be amazing.

What Is "Owning Your Sh*t"?

Owning your sh*t is about taking responsibility for all the good, bad, ugly, unknown, and indifferent pieces of your life. You cannot ignore aspects of you and expect to enjoy your life fully. It didn't work for me and I am sure it's not working for you right now. If you are ignoring some pieces of your life or are not happy with them, then you are not really living your whole life. As a result, there are days, feelings, situations, and results that suck. The only way to stop having so many shitty experiences and thoughts is to take responsibility for all parts of you and find a way to either do something different or let something go. We all know this between our ears, but we struggle to actually act on it.

There is nothing in this book you don't already know. All the answers already exist within each of us. Coming to terms with what we know and then putting that knowledge into practice is the process we struggle with. You don't create results by knowing something; results only come from acting on what you know and creating a visceral experience that you can learn from and improve on next time. This book will help clarify what you know, and offer simple ways to put that knowledge into better practice.

Owning your sh*t is first and foremost about knowing your self-worth. It is about cultivating awareness of what you uniquely bring to the world through the value you hold. Next up is combining that feeling of self-worth with a very clear understanding of what you truly want—not what others want for you or what you think you *should* want. Owning your sh*t means letting go of everything else once these two pieces are in place, because none of it matters and it will only cause further frustration, fear, and pain.

Nothing will provide you with a quick fix for your personal problems, and this book is no different. This book will, however, present some simple and universally true ideas, tips, tools, understandings, new perspectives, and stories for you to try out in your own life.

Life is found in the journey and created in the details.

Use the parts that fit for you and discard the rest. You are on your own unique journey, learning your lessons, and what works for me might not work for you. But you won't know until you try something and see the results for yourself. Life is not about being right or wrong. Life is about learning and growing, and when you focus on that, you'll continuously enjoy life while forever growing forward.

While there might not be any quick fixes, there are millions of small things along the way that help us create the outcomes we desire. Along the road of life, we face more challenges and opportunities than we ever imagined, but if we've committed to our outcome, greatness is there for the taking. The first step to making things happen and enjoying your daily life—before even realizing your true worth or gaining greater awareness of your desires—is to immediately take full responsibility for yourself. That's what owning your sh*t means. It's not a complicated idea. What might seem like an epic journey reserved for mythical heroes, leaders of industry, and professional athletes is in reality not much different for you and me. But epic journeys must begin with self-ownership—that is, with full responsibility for one's self. Only then will the principles those heroes stick to and the actions they take truly make sense to us. What we are ultimately seeking is more awesome moments—more *heroic* moments.

Owning your sh*t is about making choices right now, choices that are not guided by immediate pleasure or by ease, but rather by your longer-term wants and needs and those of the ones you care about. These choices are mostly about doing less, not more, and making small tweaks that lead to long-term differences. Large, sudden movements will only cause you to burn off your resources too quickly and will make it harder to tell what to further tweak when things change. Smaller, more consistent steps build momentum toward the outcomes you seek. Small steps may not appear sexy all the time, but they're far more likely to get you where you want and to keep it enjoyable along the way.

When you are fully committed and completely authentic, you can do anything you want. Being your authentic self doesn't mean you have all the answers, but it does build a powerful foundation for the rest of your life to grow upon. You don't need to move around the world, quit your job, give all your money away, change faiths, or dye your hair blue to be authentically you. You simply need to focus on being present and determine what is relevant for you. As you become more authentic, you will remove and add small things to your day-to-day life that will be mostly unnoticeable to other people but make a profound difference for you. I believe life is found in the journey and created in the details. Life is ebb and flow, and you have to be aware of this as it relates to you. What most people overlook in the equation of life is time. It takes time for change to occur, results to show up, lessons to be learned, meaning to be understood, and happiness to become your new norm.

Everything is always changing regardless of whether we want it to. You must know this in your bones and, instead of fighting or resisting change, go with the natural flow. This doesn't mean always taking the easy road in life. Everything in this world has a natural flow and a path of least resistance. Notice how two people dancing together flow better than two people arguing with each other. Observe the natural movement of flowing water finding the easiest path forward to create a river. Your life has the same natural flow, and when you begin looking for it and stop fighting it, changes will happen more easily and enjoyably while taking you to exactly where you need to be.

As you venture forward into the book, you'll notice it is broken into three parts. As with any good plan, it helps to start with a strong foundation to build upon, which is what the first part of the book is all about. Here you'll learn how to embrace change, how to be more authentic, how to master what it means to settle into yourself, and how listening and putting yourself first are cornerstones to owning your sh*t.

In part 2 I'll show you why asking questions is the key to knowing yourself better and being infinitely resourceful. You are already asking a lot of questions, but learning how to better shape and understand these questions is what makes all the difference.

In part 3 I'll outline the Four Stages of Making Sh*t Happen. This four-stage process of awareness, choice, action, and commitment comprise a specific process you can use to fully embrace the principles of owning your sh*t and create any result you seek. My goal throughout the book is to make things as simple as possible to understand and take action upon. That doesn't mean it's easy to do, but if something isn't simple, we don't stand a chance at doing it. Remember, taking even one idea from this will change your life.

PART I

The Foundation

Embracing Change

We all want to change something, but we're not always sure how to best navigate that process. Perhaps you dream of inventing a new mobile application, starting a small business, writing a screenplay, losing weight, going back to school, quitting your job, running a marathon, or ending your struggling relationship. But let's start smaller. I mean really small. Let's set the bar so low you could trip on it.

If you want to get fit, for example, you need to get off your ass and start exercising regularly. I know: easier said than done. But what if you started by setting a reasonable goal like fifteen pushups and a forty-five-minute walk today? The failure rate on a commitment like this is low because it's not like you have to do all the pushups or the whole forty-five-minute walk at once. Do it bit by bit throughout the day—ten minutes here, twenty minutes there, etc.—and you'll discover it wasn't as hard as you initially thought. Succeeding at such a task, no matter how small, will encourage you to reach higher tomorrow and the next day, and will eventually lead you to the result you seek.

Change is pretty easy when you think of it as simply doing something different than you are currently doing, and then steadily building on that each day. The worst thing you can do is overwhelm yourself by setting an unrealistic, immediate goal that will cause you to fail or, worse, to not even start. Keep setting that bar a little higher each day, and you will eventually find a sweet spot, a goal that's not too easy, not too hard—something you can achieve daily.

Every action you take affects the direction of your life, and you're going to start taking small, simple, positive actions now. Even if you do just one tiny thing differently, you can effect a drastically different outcome. Automatic savings plans and compound interest are great examples of this. You won't even miss the small percentage of your income you automatically invested, but it will make a big difference in a few decades when you want to retire or make a large purchase. Another example is traveling by boat. If you change the boat's direction even a couple of degrees, you could end up on a completely different continent. Consider the big difference that small things make, and work your way forward from there. We spend too much time thinking of the end result and not thinking of what we can do right now. Our obsession with the end result won't by itself provide us anything tangible or immediately actionable. It's too big to get to in a single step, so we simply don't do anything and thus fail to change at all.

Here's the awesome part about change: Since you're always changing anyway, all you have to do is better guide the changes that are currently happening. Learn to embrace and ride the wave of change instead of resisting it. Enjoy the flow of change while steering yourself in a direction that better aligns with your desires. Creating a change while riding the wave is nothing more than doing something small—consistently.

I get stuck a lot in life. Mainly it's my energy and attitude. When I am feeling low and slow and not having fun, it sucks, but I know the feelings will pass. So rather than stay stuck in my funky mood with my blah energy, I work on digging myself out—a few tweaks over an afternoon or couple of days can get me joking and smiling again. These tweaks could be anything: eating something healthy so my body is fueled well, taking an extra-long walk to the beach

---

There are tons of victories worth achieving, lessons worth learning, questions worth asking. Your task is to choose.

---

with my dog so I can get more fresh air, watching a TED Talk to get inspired. Tweak means simple. Simple is good. Simple is better than nothing. And it's definitely better than mindlessly channel surfing, oversleeping, eating garbage, isolating ourselves—all the batshit-crazy decisions we make when we're in this crappy mindset. These bad feelings will often pass—eventually. Making them pass more quickly is up to each of us.

Change is easy when life is good. Yet we usually fantasize most about changing when life challenges us, and that's when creating change requires more work and discipline. That's how life works: That thing you want or need the most is typically the hardest thing to do in that moment. It's like a test to make sure you're committed, to make sure you earn that victory. And earning that victory often takes time. Tomorrow might not be that time. Neither might the next day, or month, or even year. There might be more lessons to learn, more stories to live through, before you can earn that victory. So enjoy those lessons. Enjoy those experiences along the way. They're what make the victories worth it. There are tons of victories worth achieving, lessons worth learning, questions worth asking.

Your task is to *choose*.

Change always starts with you. You are powerful and influential: Just as your positive attitude and actions enhance the world around you, your bad attitude or unkind actions distance your friends, family, colleagues, and even total strangers. Even if you are struggling to change, interact with the world around you with kindness and integrity in order to avoid creating a negative domino effect. You will feel much more gusto and power to create a life you enjoy if you are treating other people and the world with respect.

Putting Yourself First

When I was about thirteen, I hated going on family vacation. It always meant we'd pack up the car and go hiking, canoeing, and camping around British Columbia and Alberta, Canada, for a few weeks. Places like Banff, Jasper, Lake Louise, Nelson, and Smithers. The problem was that we already lived in a small town where most of the things we did were outdoor activities anyway. I was frustrated that we couldn't go on a "real" vacation to Hawaii or Disneyland.

One weekend, my mother, father, and younger sister decided they all wanted to take a day trip to another small town for a typical family outing. I, however, did not want to go, and finally made my stand. It didn't go over too well, and I vividly remember hiding under my bed while my mother yelled at me and tried to pull me out. Somehow I held my ground and refused to leave. My parents were angry with me, but eventually they gave up and yelled, "Fine, you want to stay? You'll stay!" I now realize that this was the tipping point. I had not only won the freedom to stay home; I had made a choice to live my life on my own terms. I quickly realized that if I was going to stay home alone, I had to step up and be responsible for myself.

My parents are amazing people. One of the coolest things they taught me is that we all have to take ownership of ourselves. I knew that my newfound privilege to stay home alone was something I needed to take seriously and do right—or I wouldn't get it again. So I made good use of my first time staying home alone. I was adult about it, and I fully embraced the role of taking care of myself and the house.

> # Most of us don't put ourselves first. We put other people— and things—first. If you want to change something, you need to put *you* first.

My approach worked, because I didn't have to go on family vacation ever again. Whenever my family left for a weekend road trip, or a multiweek camping trip, I got to stay home and do my own thing. I would cook, clean, go grocery shopping, get myself to school, and get to sleep at a decent hour. The big joke became that the house, and everything around it, was in better shape when they got back than it had been when they left! I realized that independence was a privilege, not a right, and I didn't want to screw it up and risk losing it. By staying home alone I learned to become the leader in my own life because I took responsibility for myself and what I wanted. I put myself first.

Most of us don't put ourselves first. We put other people—and things—first. If you want to change something, you need to put *you* first. If you can't take care of you, then how are you going to help anyone else, be a good partner, raise a family, manage your finances, get a new job, start a business, or lose ten pounds?

The areas of your life you feel most frustrated in and are not getting the results you want in are the areas you are not putting yourself first in. Imagine if you always took responsibility, owned your sh*t, and didn't blame other people or circumstances for any part of your life. You could simply focus on creating opportunity and abundance while having fun. When we don't own our sh*t, we are operating from a place of scarcity and fear.

Whatever you do, *own* it. If you feel grumpy, *own it*. If you feel awesome, *own it*. Put yourself first and *own* your sh*t. When you own your sh*t, you are not saying everything is perfect—and you're not saying that family, friends, finances, body issues, and other factors don't influence you or sometimes hinder you—but you are embracing every aspect of yourself, being fully present, and owning the results of your life, no matter what. In other words, you aren't attributing your circumstances—failures *and* successes—to outside influences.

This also means not spending your life doing what you think other people want you to do, and instead putting your unique needs and wants first. This sounds selfish, and in a way it is, but when your needs and desires are fulfilled, you can authentically and sustainably *help others* without fear or resentment.

Being Authentic

Being authentic means living your life from the inside out, instead of from the outside in. It's about knowing who you are and getting comfortable enough with yourself to be honest and transparent. Most of us look to family, friends, pop culture, and our peers to define who we are, or to tell us who we should be. This is a great starting point, as we learn by watching and emulating those whom we admire, but eventually you'll want to customize your life to fit *you* . . . and this is where things get complicated.

Authenticity is about being unafraid to be true to yourself no matter who may, or may not, approve. It's announcing with pride, "I don't want to drink alcohol," "I am a vegetarian," "I want to be a beekeeper," "I'm gay," "I'm moving to Portland," "I quit," "I don't want to be in a relationship with you anymore," "I love you," or "I don't want to go to school right now." It's about understanding what you truly enjoy. When you live your life in congruency with what is true for you, you are on your way to happiness and success. Living authentically is, of course, a process. I remind myself all the time to just be James. There is no cookie-cutter success formula that works for everyone; we are each unique and all have to forge our own paths.

You have to face your own fears, truths, and the awkwardness that can ensue from being completely honest and fully accepting yourself. Brené Brown is an American scholar, author, and public speaker who is currently a research professor at the University of Houston Graduate College of Social Work. "Authenticity is a collection of choices that we have to make every day," she says. "It's about the choice to show up and be real. The choice to be honest. The choice to let our true selves be seen."

This means that everything we identify as awesome and worthy of pursuit comes from allowing ourselves to be vulnerable and open to other people and new experiences. Vulnerability sounds like weakness. But it's anything but. Vulnerability is at the heart of authenticity because it's about having the courage to let yourself be seen for who you are: No predetermined outcomes or perfection is required. Without the authenticity that comes from vulnerability, you'll find it difficult to connect with yourself and others—one of the ultimate reasons we're here at all—and that feeling of "looking for something in life" will never be satisfied, fueling our fears of disconnection, unworthiness, loneliness, and isolation. Being authentic is not merely embracing your originality—it's letting go of who you think you should be in order to be who you really are. Authenticity also means loving yourself unconditionally.

> # Authenticity also means loving yourself unconditionally.

Being authentic, or not, is one of the biggest obstacles that stands between where you are today and where you want to be. When you follow the authentic voice of your heart, you will end up experiencing life in a way that truly satisfies you. You have a responsibility to be true to yourself. Are you brave enough to embrace it?

Listening Actively

Learning to listen to yourself and others is one of the hardest skills to develop. Listening is a key component of owning your sh*t because as you go through the process of detoxifying your life and taking responsibility for creating your own reality you will start to see your world very differently, and listening means facing hard truths about your life up until now. Listening to yourself and the feedback you get from others—and learning how to use the information you receive—will make the difference between success and failure.

The power of listening really clicked in for me shortly before I started coaching. I used to like to talk a *lot*. I loved rambling about facts and ideas, and would talk about practically anything with anybody at any time. You could often find me in my element at networking events busily meeting new people and broadcasting myself to whoever would listen. But that started to change when I became interested in listening to what was really going on inside me.

I knew some things in my life weren't working. I knew that I needed to be quiet enough to hear what was really going on inside so I could get a better perspective on what was actually happening around me. I started reading books about personal growth, observing people who were really good leaders, listening to personal-development speakers, and attending leadership workshops. One key observation that stood out for me was that most leaders, managers and CEOs—the people in positions I sought and whom I looked up to—spent a lot of time listening. I realized I wasn't listening enough, and that if I wanted to better understand myself or anybody else, I would have to really listen first. Initially, I wasn't comfortable with listening because I didn't know what I was listening for. I started listening to myself with pen and paper. I wrote down my thoughts and ideas and then read them to hear what was really happening between my ears and in my heart. I did a lot of reflection on what I wrote.

Soon I was able to listen in real time by consciously tuning in to the conversations I was having while they occurred—listening to the thoughts inside my head, listening to the words coming out of my mouth, and listening to what people were really saying to me. I learned to speak and listen at the same time, and I found that I got so much more out of life and was able to build rapport so much faster by listening instead of just talking. I also recognized that if I ever wanted to help people, I would first need to listen to them to figure out what they were really saying before I could determine how to best help them. I made this major shift from being a talker to a listener over the course of a few months and received a lot of feedback about the drastic switch. People around me were shocked and impressed, and both friends and strangers began telling me I was a great listener and that they felt heard by me.

We all want to be heard, even if what we say isn't the best thing, or even if people don't agree with us. No one enjoys being dismissed or ignored. Feeling as if we're being heard is key to connecting with someone. I actually prefer listening to talking now. Listening is the only way to find out what's true for you, what you value, what feels authentic, and what your unique rules are for your life.

So how do you really listen? All these techniques can be done with yourself and with others:

- Ask probing questions that make others feel important, valued, and as if they themselves are being heard.
- Note nonverbal cues.
- Repeat back what you think you heard to ensure you really understand what was said.

According to the Listening Center in California, we spend about 80 percent of our waking hours communicating. We spend about half of this time listening—to people, music, television, radio, etc. About 75 percent of that time we are forgetful, preoccupied, or not paying attention. The average attention span for an adult in the United States is twenty-two seconds. We are constantly changing our focus, and this makes it difficult to listen for any significant length of time. Immediately after we hear someone speak we can only remember about half of what they said, and a few hours later we only remember 10 to 20 percent of that. Despite our lackluster listening abilities, less than 5 percent of people in the United States have actively concentrated on developing their skills in listening.

Vulnerability is at the heart of authenticity.

Learning to listen means learning how to *consciously* listen so that you can retain the information that best serves you. Listening is about extracting and distinguishing information while recognizing patterns. When you listen, you consciously and unconsciously filter information, looking for the bits you desire.

Because we are bombarded with more information than we can naturally filter, we often seek refuge by creating a personal bubble to block out, filter, and ignore as many parts of life as we can. Anything that seems like it's "too much work" usually gets blocked out because we are already so preoccupied just trying to filter through the noise from television, always-on smartphones, iPods, social media, advertisements, newspapers, radio, billboards, and many other sources.

When we block out messages and information by retreating into our personal bubbles, we also block out real human connection. Many of us broadcast ourselves to the world through blogs, tweets, status updates, headline news, sound clips, or online videos and think this is an acceptable substitution. But there is very little listening and real connecting through these mediums. Ultimately we have created more clutter that needs to be filtered or blocked out. In essence, we pile onto the problem—alienation, loneliness—that we seek to correct.

As a result of all this clutter we consume and create in our broadcast-crazy world, we have become impatient and we no longer want the whole story or idea. We seek sound bites, headlines, and hashtags. Because there is so much information to sort through, it's hard to decipher what is real and relevant.

This is where what I call "conscious listening" comes in. Conscious listening helps you filter out the noise so you can discover and focus on what is most important for you. Right now, even if you don't realize it, you are having a hard time paying attention to the authentic ideas, sounds, and spaces in your life because you are more focused on tuning in and tuning out noise than you are on developing conscious listening skills. Conscious listening helps you answer the important questions in your life; it helps you become aware of what is really happening so you can make good choices, take action, and commit to the things that are most important to you. It helps you discover what makes you happy, what you are passionate about, and whom you want in your life.

Settling into Yourself

When I turned thirty, I was able to finally be open and honest about the biggest secret I didn't even realize I was keeping—my age. It all started when I was fifteen and could grow a robust amount of facial hair and get into bars. From that moment, I stopped telling anyone my real age.

I had always been the youngest person in my circle of friends, at work, and when dating. When I was a seventeen-year-old in college, most of my classmates were in their early to mid twenties. When I was nineteen, I started working in marketing and sales. I had to quickly look and act older than I was to appear like the respected expert my colleagues and clients expected. By the time I was twenty-one, I was in charge of teams of people both younger and older than me, and I had to figure out how to conduct myself as a leader. When I decided to start coaching at age twenty-six, again I had to come across as older to be seen as an authority on what I was teaching.

It wasn't until my thirtieth birthday, when I invited about a hundred of my good friends and family to celebrate with me, that I finally had to proclaim to the world my real age. When most of these guests were shocked I was only turning thirty, I realized this fear wasn't imaginary—and I faced it head-on. The year that followed was the best year of my life, and each year continues to be better as a result of my admission. I was able to *settle into myself* and learn to just be me—free of judgment or games—when I stopped trying to be something I felt others wanted or needed me to be.

Settling into yourself is a natural by-product of your decision to own your sh*t, and it will be a daily, lifelong practice. Each time we figure out how to clear one hurdle and are ready to celebrate and rest, we seem to run into the next hurdle, and everything we just learned is challenged again to make sure we really learned it. For me a major hurdle was age; for others it's parenthood, marriage, passing of a loved one, or moving to a new city or country. But remember that settling into yourself is a trial-and-error process—as long as you're enjoying life and making incremental progress, you're on the right track.

> # Settling into yourself is a trial-and-error process—as long as you're enjoying life and making incremental progress, you're on the right track.

Everything you are doing with your life right now is about you working through the process of settling into yourself; we are each on our own journey, trying to make sense of our place in the world and to understand ourselves better. This process is the fabric of our lives, and this book is meant to help you navigate that weird, often uncomfortable personal evolution more effectively.

The fear of change is the biggest, beastliest obstacle to settling into yourself. When it comes down to it, most of us will do anything—or put up with far too much—in order to avoid making changes.

Too many of us are possessed by the idea that we need to hit rock bottom before we can find the leverage we need to get off our asses. We're often more motivated by fear than reward, which is why it frequently takes hitting rock bottom to spur us to change ourselves. But massive pain and frustration are not ideal places to create change from, which is why it's so critical to embrace the fact—right now—that your journey in life is to settle into yourself. Embrace continual change. Embrace the learning that comes from facing fears. Embrace letting go. Be open and excited over the fact that everything you do gives you the opportunity to learn something more about yourself. Vulnerability, openness, and honesty are essential here. When you find yourself struggling, hiding, or playing small, determine whether you are trying to conform or fit into an ideal you hold that is based on someone else—and not one based on who you are or what you want for yourself. This struggle is one of the biggest hurdles you must clear.

Being you in all your amazing, messy glory is the only way. When you step into this space, you settle into yourself.

Asking Better Questions to Get Better Answers

The questions we ask ourselves shape our sense of reality and our understanding of our lives. Throughout the day, we have a whole series of questions that go through our heads consciously and unconsciously. *Why doesn't my boss trust me? Why did the cashier look at me like that? Why aren't I smarter? Why aren't I married yet? Why don't I have kids by now? Why didn't I get a raise this year? Why don't I eat healthier? Why don't I watch less TV?* If you were paying attention, you would have noticed that these questions share one thing in common: They are all negative. We typically ask negative, disempowering questions of ourselves and the world around us, and that results in negative, disempowering answers. Then we get frustrated and wonder why our lives aren't the way we want them to be. It's a vicious cycle. The good news is that we can break the cycle and begin to create change in our lives by reframing the negative questions we ask ourselves into positive, empowering, actionable questions. Sometimes questions only need slight tweaking in order to elicit a more useful response:

Negative question: Why doesn't my boss trust me?

Positive question: What do I need to do to build trust between my boss and me?

Simply reframing the question completely changes the answer you are going to get, and this answer will create a different feeling, which will cause you to take a different action.

Why do we ask ourselves low-quality questions? We tend to paint our reality in a way that is digestible and comfortable for us to deal with and that supports our belief system. If you're asking low-quality questions, it means that your current state of thinking and how you see the world is not yet strong. You are being cynical, playing small, and coming from a place of scarcity.

It's common sense: Bad questions prelude bad answers and lead you to shitty results that you cannot use to move forward. Good questions—especially specific ones relevant to your immediate circumstances—help you take action in a positive direction. You'll know that you are asking a good question because a good question evokes *an empowering, actionable response that is within your power and not dependent on external circumstances or another person.* When you ask a positive question, you may not get the answer that you want, but you will get an answer—an accurate and revealing one—that can help you move forward. As Peter Thomson, an expert in communication, says, "Ask yourself the easy questions and you'll have a hard life; ask yourself the hard questions and you'll have an easier life."

What kind of questions are you asking yourself? Are they rhetorical? Open-ended? Do you ask them in a curious or judgmental way? For example, let's say you start to walk over to a great guy or gal to ask them to be your date for an upcoming party, but you get nervous and end up just walking past them with a quick "Hi." You could ask yourself bad questions like *Why am I such an idiot?* or *Why can't I get a date?* and set yourself up for a negative, disempowering answer that will leave you date-less and feeling like crap. Or you could ask yourself a better question, like *Why am I nervous about asking someone out?* The answer might be *Because I'm afraid of rejection*, which leads to questioning why you're afraid of rejection. There's no way to know if you'll be rejected or accepted unless you ask, and rejection's temporary sting pales in comparison to the empowerment and skill of being able to act on your desires whenever you want. When you ask yourself good, compassionate questions and listen for honest answers, you create unlimited opportunities for yourself, not to mention make yourself immediately feel lighter and more empowered. The truth, however dark or difficult, will always empower you.

> **You'll know that you are asking a good question because a good question evokes an empowering, actionable response that is within your power and not dependent on external circumstances or another person.**

In the next part of the book we'll explore the kinds of questions that plague your thoughts and cause you to go in circles. We'll break down a few key questions you need to be asking in order to break free and open up new opportunities. You must get into the habit of asking yourself positive, actionable questions—the results they will produce in your life will astound you!

PART II

The Key Questions

What Positive Did I Learn?

Failure, success, and happiness mean slightly different things for everyone. If you have failed, struggled, or suffered, you have choices. You can focus on your pain and watch it continue, loop, and get worse, or you can ask yourself one simple question: *What positive did I learn?* What did you learn about life, or about yourself, that will make life better for you, and others, now and in the future?

One of the most difficult things I've been through in my life is heartbreak. We've all been there. For me, it was the end of a five-and-a-half-year relationship. Like most relationships that don't work out, we had both long started to compromise our own integrity and wants, and we began to grow apart in small ways. The catalyst that started the end was when she wanted to move back to the city she grew up in. She was frustrated with her work situation where we lived in Vancouver and had an opportunity to move home for a good job with her family business. I wasn't excited to move because I was quite happy with my life in Vancouver. However, I loved her and wanted to support her so decided I would be all in—fully commit—and move to Toronto with her. I knew that either we were going to get married and live happily ever after (which I was hoping for), or we were going to end very soon.

I had been in Toronto a grand total of one week when I started to feel like something wasn't right between us. We were unpacking and setting up our new apartment one afternoon. She had been quiet most of the day and I knew her well enough not to press. She would talk to me when she was ready. As I slowly unpacked the boxes, she continued to sit there silently and awkward before looking up at me. She said, "I don't want to be with you anymore. I don't think I'm in love with you. I think I'm in love with my ex-boy-friend. I'm really sorry."

> **When you focus on the positive of any situation, you are empowering yourself to move forward and create something new—something you enjoy!**

Her words hit me like a giant truck. I had just completely uprooted my life to be with this woman and all of a sudden she was in love with someone else? But I had come to Toronto with the intention of discovering where this relationship was headed, and in that moment I learned that I was *really* good at manifesting things! I thought it would take a while to get my answer. Who knew it would take a week?

Shocked by the words that just came out of her mouth, I asked, "Okay, try again. What's the real problem?" She just wasn't happy, she explained—which I already knew, after all. This was the root of why she had moved back to Toronto. I was hoping there was a path forward for us together, but my gut knew there wasn't, and this simply confirmed it. We weren't meant to be. Once she decided to end things, I had to live with that. I knew I didn't want to be with someone whom I had to convince to be with me.

Still, there I was in a new city. I didn't have a job, I didn't have any new business in Toronto yet, and my only possessions were two suitcases and my dog, Carter. It had taken me three months to prepare for the move to Toronto and now—plans be damned—I had to instantly figure out where to go from here: Stick it out in Toronto, or head back home?

A week later I made my choice: I returned to Vancouver and got my old life back, but it was new and improved. I renovated and refurnished my old place. I got my old job back after my original replacement left. My business started to take off even further in both cities, and everything else that I'd left came back to me better than ever.

So what positive did I learn from my two weeks in Toronto? It was truly one of the most spectacular and crazy events of my life—and I would do it over and over again because when you put yourself all in and get run over, an amazing opportunity for growth emerges. Sure, I could have crumbled and painted myself into a smaller, tighter, more depressing corner—but how would that have helped me? I learned that I could be all in, get hit, and still end up on my feet.

When you focus on the positive of any situation, you are empowering yourself to move forward and create something new—something you enjoy! This doesn't mean that the negative parts don't exist. It just means you are reframing the meaning of your experiences in constructive ways, learning new lessons, and preventing yourself from repeating the same mistakes.

Keep asking yourself the simple question: *What positive did I learn?* Take the answer and use it to do something different and better next time—no matter how many more next times—until you get the result you desire.

Am I as Overwhelmed as I Think I Am?

Imagine you've just been dropped into the middle of the ocean with nothing around you. You're flailing and panicking as waves crash over you. You can't see the shore, it's raining, there are no boats around, and it's starting to get dark. You're fighting for survival, and you don't know if you're going to make it. You're exhausted! Now, imagine if you knew that you would survive. Everything then changes: When you know that you will make it back to shore, you can calm down and focus on figuring out a plan to get there.

Life rarely throws us—literally—into the middle of an ocean. It never puts anything in front of us that we can't handle (we wouldn't be here right now if it did). But we often feel overwhelmed anyway—perhaps it's a new job, a relationship that doesn't work, bills we can barely pay, or two weddings we need to attend in the next month that we can't afford gifts for and don't have time for. Our focus and our resources continue to be drawn and quartered, and often we know we need to do something different but aren't sure what it is or how to do it. We get paralyzed and panic.

But when we realize we're not going to literally drown and that we can handle everything life is giving us—knowing it truly, in our hearts and in our bodies, not just between our ears—we all of a sudden feel empowered and resourceful. The mountain that was once daunting now looks like an interesting challenge. The journey of life—not just its destinations—looks enjoyable.

Remind yourself often that you are resilient and infinitely resourceful.

Think about hindsight. The challenges you've gone through in the past may have once seemed impossible, but you got through them because you *always* get through them. Human beings are incredibly resilient, but in the middle of a challenge, we often don't feel resilient and resourceful. *Remind yourself often that you are resilient and infinitely resourceful.* When you calm down, and stop flailing and worrying about drowning, then you can use your common sense to create a plan, solve the challenges in front of you, and move forward.

Remember, you are not going to drown. You are going to get out of the tough situation you're in and be better than you were before. But first, calm down and take a deep breath.

What Is Mirroring Back to Me?

The world is a great mirror. It reflects back to you what you are. If you are loving, if you are friendly, if you are helpful, the world will prove loving and friendly and helpful to you. The world is what you are.

—Thomas Dreier

Each person we meet is mirroring back a part of ourselves. If you see somebody doing something you don't like, instead of judging them, getting angry, or being frustrated, try asking yourself, *What is being mirrored back to me about a part of myself?*

This means we have endless opportunities to discover who we are and what we need to work on within ourselves. If your partner can't communicate clearly with you, then you probably have some work to do around clear communication yourself. If charming, fun people surround you, then you are probably in touch with and expressing these qualities yourself. If you are not happy with the circumstances you find yourself in, then you have some inner work to do before your reality will shift outside of you. Looking at other people is the best place to learn about ourselves. We tend to see things more clearly in others than we do in ourselves, and the advice we often give to others is advice that we should take ourselves.

Have I Really Grown Up Yet?

When we turn certain ages, we are granted specific privileges: driving a car, having a credit card, drinking at a bar. Age, however, is not necessarily indicative of adulthood.

Your parents will always be your parents, but they won't always tell you to go to bed or get up, to apologize, to do your laundry, to go to work, to pay your bills on time, or to eat your vegetables. Most of us figure this out in our twenties, and usually in our *late* twenties. But some of us never figure it out and remain perpetually immature and trapped by our need for someone else to help take care of us. At some point, we need to become our own parent (which really means becoming an adult) and do these things for ourselves.

This sounds so obvious—but then why are there so many people in their twenties and early thirties today who feel frustrated and do not understand what they could have done differently? They did everything "right": good grades, extracurricular achievements, college degrees. Yet they've still managed to end up buried under piles of debt, working at a local bar, holding a fancy degree while considering a move back home to save money.

One big part of the problem—the economic part—is that the

rules of the workforce changed as we grew up. The dot-com crash and the stock market crash almost a decade later turned the job landscape on its head. We are entering the workforce with record amounts of debt, into an extremely competitive job environment that is changing daily. We have been trying to afford the kind of lifestyle we might have been accustomed to growing up, the kind of lifestyle we were told we could have, too. But we are left wondering how to make it happen. The reality doesn't match the expectations we were sold.

The other big part of the problem is a cultural one. Like most generations, we in Generation Y—those, including me, born between 1979 and 1997—are stereotyped by our negative characteristics. We have become known for being entitled, self-centered, and irresponsible and for having a lack of understanding for how the world functions. While negative Gen Y stereotypes apply to many of us, they also apply to some people of every generation. Besides, almost every generation puts down the generations that have come before it, at least before that new generation takes hold of the financial power in a country. In any case, these expectations and attitudes with which we're stereotyped were instilled in us during childhood and they were nurtured by the systems we were raised in.

Two key cultural shifts happened when we were growing up. First was the idea of "self-esteem." Self-esteem was the big, vogue parenting concept during the '80s and '90s, and it resulted in most kids being constantly appreciated: "Just because you're you!" In practice, it involved frequently praising children, not criticizing them under any circumstance, emphasizing feelings, and not recognizing one child's achievements as superior to another's. At the end of a sports season, for instance, every player "won" a trophy regardless of his or her contributions to the team.

Second, our parents noticed that financial freedom and job

security depended more heavily than ever on higher education. So they pushed us on the path to get ahead by following the new set of rules. By ensuring our education and achievements, our parents hoped to give us the life they wanted and had been working so hard to provide us. They became hyper-involved, and as a result, many Gen Y-ers became accustomed to having their parents help them at each and every turn.

> **An important part of owning your sh*t is asking yourself if you are being your own parent and holding yourself accountable.**

We couldn't fail, and were always striving for more or looking for the next reward. Everything was focused on getting the best grades in school so that we could go to the best colleges, get the best jobs, make a big salary, and seize that partnership more quickly. The reality, we learned, was much different: "What do you mean I can't start as a manager? I was told if I went to college . . ."

Despite all that, Generation Y is not a negative force; we are simply our own force. We're also characterized by our optimism, our collaboration, our drive, and our philanthropy. But in order to truly embody *those* traits, the first thing we must do is stop blaming cultural and economic circumstances—circumstances that we had or have little or no control of. Understanding those circumstances is one thing. But living by them will make us die by them.

If you haven't already made the shift from adolescence to maturity, then it's time. An important part of owning your sh*t is asking yourself if you are being your own parent and holding yourself accountable. *Am I stepping up and managing all areas of my life? Do I* *still need someone to cook for me, clean for me, do my laundry, help me find a job, and be the mediator between my friends or employer and me? Am I capable of figuring all these things out on my own?* Figuring it all out may take trial and error, but it must be done if you want to own your sh*t.

Where Are My Boundaries?

We all have a boss-from-hell story, and mine occurred when I was just starting in the advertising industry. I was a junior account executive at a medium-size ad agency and excited to be working in the field I had studied and made sacrifices to enter. Like everyone who starts out in a new job, I was trying to gain as much experience as I could. That's why when we're just starting out, we don't consider what our boundaries are, and we often have to end up getting pushed to a breaking point before we learn how important they are in all areas of life— especially in careers.

The man who owned the advertising agency was really good at a few things, which obviously created a certain level of success in his business, but his success was massively limited by his unpredictable behavior and brutal people skills. He was an emotionally volatile tyrant. One moment he was screaming his throbbing red face off at me, and the next moment he was sending me on a company-paid vacation or giving me something nice to make up for his bad behavior. He would never apologize or learn from an inappropriate incident but would simply try to make it up to his staff by buying us off. A lot of people crumpled under him and were reduced to tears;

others became extremely frustrated and quit. I was eventually one of those people, but not until my boundaries were crossed.

After working a whole week of long hours on a new business-development project that was another "make more work" project from our boss, we all had a meeting to see the work we had developed. It was another random bad-mood morning for him and he lit us up in a screaming critique of the work we'd done. There was nothing constructive in his yelling, and he completely disregarded the solid effort we had put into the project. He paced around the room like an angry hippo. He was walking past me when he stopped and turned to yell directly in my face. As he stood towering above me, all I felt was tired and numb, and in that moment I lost the last bit of respect and appreciation I had for him and could no longer see any reason for being there. He had crossed a boundary; it was over. I couldn't wait to get out. My learning experience was complete. I had a new job two months later. I learned a lot from my "boss from hell," and I appreciate my experience with him for that—but I decided then to never subject myself to that kind of work environment, or any situation like it, ever again.

We must define our boundaries, stick to them, and then communicate them to other people through our words and actions. When we aren't clear about our boundaries, we run the risk of living lives we don't like, and we let other people invade our space, which frustrates us and fills us with resentment. When you set up boundaries and communicate them in a way that others clearly understand and can respect, you can confidently and empathetically say, "Yes, I know you have lots of work, but so do I and I am not going to take on your project, too."

Once you set better boundaries, you will then need to establish and communicate consequences for crossing them. When we were kids, our parents told us not to pick on our baby sister or not to break curfew. If we did, there were clearly communicated consequences for crossing those boundaries. They couldn't control our actions, but they could communicate their boundaries and the consequences for crossing them. We were always unhappy with being punished, but we knew it was going to happen, and through these situations we learned to understand boundaries and consequences.

You must define and negotiate all the terms of a boundary in advance so that when a situation arises, you can instantly implement the plan of action. This informs all parties involved of the boundaries and consequences before they adhere to or test them.

> # Often, boundaries and the consequences for crossing them are not obvious or communicated.

When you're establishing new boundaries, you *must* execute their consequences for breaking/crosing them with complete confidence and consistency or else the boundaries aren't real. Implement your boundaries calmly, rather than becoming emotional and overexplaining yourself. In the heat of the moment, if you don't have a plan, you will default to your current state, which may keep you from creating the result you are seeking.

Often, boundaries and the consequences for crossing them are not obvious or communicated. These hidden boundaries are very dangerous, as they often lie in the areas of our lives that we don't understand well and perpetually struggle with. Over time we become fearful and twitchy as they slowly but surely alter our behaviors and thoughts. We begin accommodating others in ways that run counter to our goals and values. Essentially, we keep surrendering pieces of ourselves—without being able to articulate why or even being able to recognize we're doing it at all. This is how we create people like my old boss, how we turn others into monsters with no respect for boundaries. It's also how we ourselves end up like those people. Don't let that happen: Articulate your boundaries and the consequences for trespassing them, and keep looking to develop boundaries and consequences in areas of your life where you need them most.

Where's My Focus?

Whatever you focus on defines you. This is why people can have such vastly different opinions about their surroundings. If you focus on the fact that you hate your job and that it's the worst eight hours you spend in a day, then I guarantee that every day at your job will suck—and the results of your work will reflect your focus. Quitting this job you proclaim to hate might seem like the best answer, but it probably isn't. The quick, short-term solution is to change your focus about your job before you write the whole thing off. Changing your focus can make all the difference. If you still don't like your job after you have adjusted your focus, then at least you can say you tried. Remember: Wherever you go, there you are. If you bring a shitty attitude or focus to your job, to your relationships, or even to grocery shopping, your experience will be negatively affected.

We spend too much of our day focused on the negative. This tendency causes us to perceive reality as shitty and disempowering. Take an inventory of what you focus on, and think about, throughout the day. Are you focused on judging? Are you frustrated and playing small in life? Are you focused on pain and struggle? Or are you focused on joy, things that inspire you, people you love, and the opportunities for growth? When you choose a better focus, you change how you experience life, even when nothing appears to have changed externally. The cool thing is that when you make your focus positive and empowering, your external reality will begin to shift to match it.

Author David Foster Wallace once said in a college commencement speech: "The point is that petty, frustrating crap like this is exactly where the work of choosing is gonna come in. Because the traffic jams and crowded aisles and long checkout lines give me time to think, and if I don't make a conscious decision about how to think and what to pay attention to, I'm gonna be pissed and miserable every time I have to shop." When you learn to master your focus, you will be able to shape and reshape your world at any given moment, create new meaning within your daily thoughts and actions, and stop feeling as if you are out of control or at the mercy of the world outside you.

> **When you make your focus positive and empowering, your external reality will begin to shift to match it.**

Am I Actively Designing My Life?

We have been developing our own specific blueprints since we were born, and they continue to grow and change with age. Our blueprints contain all the technical specifics for how we'd like our lives to look overall. As we get older we become more aware of our blueprint. When our reality matches our blueprints, we are happy and consider our lives successful and fun. When they don't match, we tend to look at ourselves as failures.

Let's say your blueprint for fitness and health includes going to the gym three days a week for forty-five minutes at a time, doing one hour of yoga daily, and eating vegetarian. To some people, this might seem completely unrealistic. For others, forty-five minutes at the gym might just be a warm-up. We each define what health looks like to us in our own unique blueprint. It's important to recognize that you will feel healthy and congruent when your reality matches the blueprint you've sketched for yourself. This congruency will have you feeling strong, empowered, and confident.

Let's say your diet is only so-so. You only make it to yoga a couple of times a month, and you get to the gym once or twice on a good week. When your reality doesn't match your physical-health blueprint, you will inevitably feel unhealthy and frustrated. Unless you want to continue feeling this way, you have to do one of two things: Change your blueprint to meet your reality, or build a reality that matches your blueprint. You can also do a bit of both; but if you want to feel as if you are living up to your expectations of yourself, you must find a way to make your blueprint and reality match. When you leave your daily actions up to chance, you often end the day with regret, frustration, and stress. If you're building, repairing, and maintaining a reality that matches your blueprint, each day will be more successful than the last.

> **You will feel healthy and congruent when your reality matches the blueprint you've sketched for yourself.**

How Do I Know When to Make the "Last Call"?

A "last call" is when you do something that you know is no longer working for you or that you no longer want in your life *for the very last time*. You can think of it as the final drink you order before you're done for the night. It's that one last pack of cigarettes, that one last night you stay up until three in the morning playing video games, that one last meaningless relationship before you finally let the habit go and learn the lesson.

Last calls acknowledge the gap between where you are and where you want to be, and let you double-check your decision one last time before you take the leap to the new and better thing for you. Last calls work because they give us the final piece of leverage, that last bit of closure, or a physical reminder that we need to make the decision to change. Sometimes you may want to make a change, but you aren't totally sure that you're done with the old habit. Perhaps something you've done for a long time doesn't fit with new goals you're working toward. Having a last call with these old habits and patterns removes the doubt that you might have and allows you to happily step into the new habit or goal with no regret or feeling of "what if." If you are unsure or second-guessing how you feel about something, then have a last call, get your answer, and move on. If you're curious about whether you truly want to keep doing something, then simply check and see by trying it again.

I recently made a last call with a girl I had a huge crush on. I had known her for a few months and liked her from the moment we met. But after knowing each other for a few months, my feelings waxed and waned on wanting to date her. Finally, there came a point where I knew that I needed to let go of the idea of anything other than a friendship with her. In order to do this I still had some lingering questions and feelings in my head and heart so I needed to hang out with her one more time one-on-one to get these questions answered and confirm the thing I knew—we were not a good intimate match and she wasn't who I wanted to be with. I needed that last call in order to push up against both what I knew to be true and the ideas I was trying to let go of. I no longer have those feelings toward her and she is a great friend in my life.

How Do I "Manage the Gap"?

Remember the girl who unceremoniously dumped me after I moved to Toronto to be with her—who, in effect, made her own "last call" on me? The hardest part about that situation was trying not to let my ego get the best of me: Why hadn't she chosen *me*? We all want to feel wanted, and when this girl said there was somebody else, my ego took over and searched for ways to "win." There was a battle going on inside me between my ego and my real self: I knew the breakup was for the best but was struggling to accept it.

We had been together for over five years, and then suddenly we weren't. When I found myself three thousand miles away back in Vancouver, I had to find a way to deal with the emotional aftermath of the breakup. I knew that we didn't fit best together, but I craved the connection and routine we shared. If I wanted to move forward, I had to figure out how to *manage the gap* between where I was then and where I wanted to be now. I had to take what had happened and find a way to choose it as my own reality. Only then could I own the result and be in a place to pick myself up and be all in again. I worked on changing my focus and giving the situation a new meaning, and that led me to taking new action. But while I was living it, the gap was a very uncomfortable place to be. What made it bearable was that I knew it was the only way through. You cannot shortcut a gap. You must learn to manage the gap and exist in the uncomfortable moments in order to come to terms with the reality and move forward.

Managing the gap is also really important for anyone who has ever lost a job. This usually happens suddenly—one moment you have a job, and the next you don't. When we lose a job, we're left wondering what to do next and how to make money to support our lives. The loss of a job and the loss of a relationship can both be painful experiences. When change like this occurs, however, it's almost always because the person or job (or any other experience you previously had in your life) wasn't really what you wanted, and is not the best fit for you. Sure, aspects of him/her/it may have been what you wanted, such as the comfort of connection with a partner or the support of a regular paycheck—and that's where you have to manage the gap. You had the comfort of the paycheck, or a warm body in your bed, and now you don't have this thing or person anymore and there is a gaping hole that you have to deal with in order to get that result again.

Remember, wonderful and exciting things happen in the gap between two trapezes.

It's important to realize that you're only experiencing a gap between when you had those things and when you'll have them again, and in that gap you have the opportunity to discover something or someone that aligns far better with what you really desire. In the meantime, you must find a way to come to terms with your current situation, own your sh*t, choose the result as your own, and take empowering action to move forward and be and do better. Remember, wonderful and exciting things happen in the gap between two trapezes.

How Do I Handle Judgment?

I love to sing and dance when I drive, run, work, or walk my dog, yet I am not very good at either of them. Still, that doesn't stop me. I never used to be comfortable enough to do this, but now I do it in hopes that people see me and smile. To me that is a victory. Actions like these create change in the world at the micro level, which is how every macro change begins.

But we never create the changes we seek if we let our judgments rule our lives. It doesn't take much skill or bravery to judge others and ourselves. Judgment is simply feeling like we are not good enough.

The worst judgments we make are the ones we make on the thoughts or ideas in our own head. These self-judgments hold us back from expressing ourselves and taking risks that give us the chance to grow. We have been conditioned to be "normal," and anything that doesn't fit "normal" we judge. We fear being abnormal because that would mean we are different and don't fit into the group. A human being's main survival technique is being part of a group, so anything that challenges that ability is a primal survival worry. However, a major part of owning our sh*t is figuring out which group we fit into. Our conditioning and environment have informed us of what might be expected of us, but the judgment creeps in when we are not sure whether those expectations match our desires.

In order to move beyond this, throw caution to the wind and ignore that inner voice of self-judgment and fear of not being "normal." Listen to your body, rather than the endless negative chatter of your mind, to gauge what makes you feel awesome. This may make you feel awkward, look silly, or stand out. Perfect—that's the real you! Rock it out loud and proud and you'll be amazed at how it actually connects you to other people in better-fitting groups rather than separates you. Many people will smile and laugh with you, and appreciate you for being unabashed and putting it out there. These are the kind of people that are fun and supportive. They are the people you want to know and have around. Overriding your judgment allows you to see who and what is real and awesome in your world and let go of the rest.

It often feels like we are each waiting for someone to give us permission to let our realness out—quirks and all. This is what you're looking for anyway and it's just beyond the point you're at right now. The best part is that when you go first and own your sh*t, it will inspire someone else to do the same and create a domino effect of awesomeness in your world.

I want to be honest with you: no matter how much you ignore the voice of judgment in your head; it is never going to fully go away. The good news is that this can actually be used in your favor. You can use that little (okay, sometimes *huge*) voice of judgment you have as a gauge to show you where your "edges" are. Edges are the places at the end of your comfort zone. It's in these places that we can grow and learn the most. When judgment speaks up, be excited and listen to what it says and use it as an opportunity to learn and grow. It is a tool to help you get closer to the *you* that you want to be. Don't let judgment cage you in a scared, awkward version of yourself. Judgment is simply a marker to show you your current edges and boundaries so you can focus on expanding your life and being better.

Judgment is fed by silence and fear. It cannot survive in truth and light. I used to be afraid of being in the light, afraid that everyone would find out the truth about me. I was sure that I was alone in the darkness and that all my secrets and fears were crazy and that I wasn't worth the air I breathed. I used to think that I was broken. I used to believe that something was inherently wrong with me. I thought that by being the person others deemed cool, fun, interesting, smart, sexy, and successful I could get rid of the ugly parts of me. I used to think that by starving myself, I could shed the weight of my humanity, or that if I stayed silent nobody would notice the scared and ugly parts of me. I know now that that was the judgment speaking. The truth was revealed when I started to exercise my ability to speak up and understand the judgment. Today I have the courage to say what's on my mind and act how I feel, knowing that judgment will be passed by others and myself. It no longer stops me. I can transform my judgment through understanding, and someone else's judgment of me is not my concern or even my business.

The "cure" to judgment is to meet it with understanding. What is the root of the judgmental thought or belief? As I mentioned,

> **Judgment is simply a marker to show you your current edges and boundaries so you can focus on expanding your life and being better.**

judgment won't stop happening, but it will be transformed when met with understanding. Once you have compassionately explored the root of a judgment, take the type of action you really want to take despite any fears. Sing out loud to your favorite song while driving with friends! You will feel liberated, and will probably be pleasantly surprised by your friends as they chime in over time.

Am I Doing Too Much?

No one is simply looking to do more stuff in his or her everyday life, but we are all looking to be more efficient so that we can do the things that matter most to us—fun things like spending more time with friends or family, reading, playing sports, traveling, camping, writing, or learning to play the guitar.

But now that we all have things like email, text messaging, and Skype, we aren't necessarily more efficient—we just do more work. We communicate more, and rely less on planning, integrity, and independent thinking. People take less responsibility for themselves, and we overcommunicate by constantly checking in and expecting people to do things at all hours. We are piling onto the problem—when we should be trying to solve it.

When we get caught up on this "doing treadmill" of stuff, it's hard to be aware of what brings us joy, let alone find the time to discover it. We become so focused on doing all the stuff on our daily checklist that the things that matter most get eternally postponed. *I just need to get through this meeting/list/day/week/month/quarter—then I'll have some free time.* This kind of thinking follows what is called the "if/then model," which will only keep you on the treadmill and take you away from actively creating the life you want.

When you have free time to do nothing—to just be—life will come over you like a wave. You may feel peaceful and gain clarity, or you may feel anxiety that you should be doing something else, but either way you will become attuned to what emotions you are really experiencing and where you are in your life. This is when your authentic thoughts come through. Maybe you'll remember that you haven't written or painted in a long time. Maybe you'll realize you want to redecorate your house, start baking, or make homemade Christmas cards this year. The sure way to this kind of clarity is doing *less*, not more. Communicating less, making fewer lists, and sometimes even having less money can actually get you the success and happiness you want.

> **By doing less, you open up space in your life for more free time, friends, and fun.**

By doing less, you open up space in your life for more free time, friends, and fun. The people who are at the top of what they do aren't always working or "doing" all the time. They are the ones who can master the few truly essential tasks that are required each day and use the rest of their time to stay inspired, connect with people, and stay healthy and creative. Doing less takes efficiency, focus, and clear boundaries. Doing less is the only way to get off the "doing treadmill" so you can free up time and space in your life to see—and then do— what you truly enjoy.

How Do I Define Success?

Years ago I was struggling to define success for myself. I used to set ridiculous goals and ideals that I was going to work toward and most of them never amounted to anything. I would lose momentum rather quickly and get frustrated because I was trying to figure out what success meant to me. I found that I was basing it on what I saw others calling success, and so I emulated them. As I know now, basing it off of other people never works. Even after I clarified my ideas of success, I found my resolve fading as things got tough and mundane. It wasn't until I looked at it from a different perspective that I started to make real progress. Instead of focusing so much on the big picture, I focused on feeling successful in the short term. As I began to examine my version of success in more detail, I realized that what made me feel successful was not necessarily achieving the end goal of a big project. End goals only happen once and for a brief moment. I need to feel successful now, over and over again, and that feedback and momentum keeps me focused and moving forward toward the end result.

I discovered the key to success is to take action every day that steers you toward your goals. I know people talk about this all the time, but once you discover it for yourself, there really is no truer motto. If you are taking daily action that moves you toward what you seek in life, then you are moving forward *regardless* of your pace. Consistently moving forward an inch is a much more effective strategy than taking massive action that's followed by frustration, burnout, and massive inaction. That's a roller-coaster experience that yields little to no results, and eventually, you need to get off the ride.

> **The key to success is to take action every day that steers you toward your goals.**

Once I got off the ride, I realized that any type of forward progress is success. Simply doing something each day that moved me toward my goals was the key. I learned to set more realistic daily goals that allowed me to accomplish everything I needed to in a day to feel successful. The pressure of having to create giant results each day and the stress over it was alleviated. This means that some days I'm happy with just an email or conversation, while other days are filled with hours of work. All days can be successful with small daily action.

As you move into part 3 and start working step by step toward change, remember that there is a universal gestation period that is required before you can experience results. It takes time to change your current habits, so give results time to appear. We spend most of our time reaching for our goals, not basking in the final result. So as you're reaching, don't spend so much time focusing on the end result that you miss the joy that can be found in your day-to-day progress—that's where the learning and growth happen.

PART III

The Four Stages

The Four Stages of Making Sh*t Happen

We all want to make things happen in our lives, but we often struggle to figure out *how* to do so. And while the principles of owning your sh*t we've covered so far are great, it's putting them into practice that takes the most work.

The fact is, right now you're probably already using some type of process to help you decide everything from what to make for dinner to whether you should start a business, drive or walk to work, go on a vacation, or marry a particular person. But this "process" is probably more like a group of scattered thoughts, attitudes, and behaviors that aren't clearly defined, understood, or followed consistently. In other words, it's a recipe for inconsistent results. That's where the Four Stages of Making Sh*t Happen come in.

The Four Stages comprise a specific process you can use to fully embrace the principles of owning your sh*t. This process prepares you to "manage the gap" between where you are and where you want to be by helping you find the natural flow of your life and channel that flow into the consistent and desired outcomes you want, with as little negative stress as possible.

So how do the Four Stages work? Think about it this way: When you build a puzzle, do you take one random piece out of the box at a time and try to find a fit for that individual piece, without even knowing what the puzzle picture is supposed to look like? Of course not. We start with the simplest, most obvious steps first. We take all the pieces out of the box at once. Then we sort them. We find the corners, the edges, and the similar colors. We use the picture on the front of the box as a point of reference. Eventually, a completed puzzle that matches the picture comes together. You can put the pieces of your life together in much the same way by using the Four Stages of Making Sh*t Happen.

Stage One: Awareness. This is where you take all the pieces of the puzzle out of the box, lay them out, and get an idea of what the puzzle's supposed to look like. Awareness is about making a conscious effort to identify and understand the current realities of your life. It's about asking yourself the tough questions—and not hiding from the sometimes tough answers.

Stage Two: Choice. From there, it's your choice whether or not you want to build this puzzle. You need sufficient awareness to say "I choose" and make empowered, creative choices to move forward in the specific direction you want.

Stage Three: Action. This is the *doing* stage. Here you create an action plan, a road map to the destination you have chosen. (That's what we do with the puzzle when we start finding the four corners and all the edges and then group similar colors together.) Making your move is about assigning actionable steps to the choices you made. You start with the end result in mind—the puzzle picture on the box, in other words—and then work backward to figure out what needs to be done or considered in order to get to that end result. If you're a musician, for example, this could mean starting by imagining the feeling of you playing your finished song to an audience who loves it, and then deciding what it'll take, specifically, to get there.

Stage Four: Commitment. If you give up part way through building your own personal puzzle, or fail to learn from your mistakes, or aren't able to embrace the uncomfortable moments between starting and finishing, you won't ever get results.

When you follow this four-stage process of awareness, choice, action, and commitment (and don't skip any stages or mix up their order), you exponentially increase your chances of getting the results you want.

DISCLAIMER

If what you're thinking right now is I *know* all this, you're not ready. These three words stunt growth instantly. If you are not prepared to be fully honest with yourself, you're not ready. Of all the lies, the ones we tell ourselves are often the worst. And if you are easily distracted or aren't ready to make real changes in your life no matter how big or small, you are—you guessed it—not ready. You must be ready to be uncomfortable and to look at your life from all angles and make new decisions and take new actions in the moment. You must be willing to fail and get right back up and do it again differently. You have to be fully committed to getting the results you want. You will need to free your life of distractions and make tough choices and build new routines.

To those who *are* ready: I'm not promising that it will be easy—you should run from anyone who does—but it will be simple, and it will provide you with the framework to transform your thinking and give you the results you desire. You will learn to take all the negative garbage crammed between your ears and replace it with inspiring, authentic ideas, words, thoughts, and feelings.

The only question left to consider before you jump in is: Are you really committed? If so, let's get started!

HIT THE GROUND RUNNING

Like every process, the Four Stages of Making Sh*t Happen have best practices. No matter what results you're looking to create, having a solid foundation to build from will only help strengthen the process and will put you ahead of the game. So before you start I have four tips to help you improve your results.

Tip 1: Remove Distractions

Free up space for new ideas and opportunities to flow in. Try temporarily adopting at least three to five of the following practices:

- Stop watching television or randomly surfing the Internet and social media sites.
- Stop consuming news media on television, radio, newspapers, blogs, and websites.
- Stop drinking, doing recreational drugs, smoking, eating junk food, and having sex with someone that isn't your long-term partner.
- Don't buy anything new unless it's a basic need.
- Stop consuming pornography.
- If you're single, stop dating, and if you're in a relationship, set alone-time boundaries and space away from your partner.
- Stop hanging out with negative people and being in negative situations.

- Remove everything inauthentic from your life and replace it with something real. This goes for food, people, information, entertainment, conversations, thought processes, and anything else you can think of.
- Stop multitasking.

Tip 2: Clean Up
Cleaning up things that have been lying around or that you've been procrastinating on will help free up mental and physical space. Try some of the following activities:
- Clean your house, office, and car, and keep them that way.
- Pay any outstanding bills.
- Return any remaining phone calls or emails.
- Pick up, drop off, or return anything that has been lingering.
- Groom yourself: Get a haircut, shave/wax, manicure/pedicure, or whatever makes you feel polished.

Tip 3: Build New Habits
Adding some of these new habits and routines into your life will help create momentum and energy for you to make sh*t happen.
- Set up a daily and weekly schedule of chores, commitments, and tasks.
- Go to bed and get up at specific times.
- Get physical by doing at least thirty minutes of exercise five days a week:
  - Join a gym, run, practice yoga, start a boot camp, or join a sports team.
  - Get outside as much as possible.
- Talk with people face to face as much as possible.
- Drink lots of water to keep your body hydrated.
- Daydream and practice being creative.

Tip 4: Follow Through

Once you start something, stick with it. Remember to do the following:

- Push yourself into the uncomfortable zone, beyond your limits.
- Once you start, don't stop. It's restarting that is the hardest part.
- Create forward progress every day.
- Make notes of when times are hard and when times are good so you can see the patterns and do more of the good and figure out how to shortcut the bad.

STAGE ONE
Awareness

"Would you tell me, please, which way I ought to go from here?"
said Alice.

"That depends a good deal on where you want to get to,"
said the Cat.

"I don't much care where—" said Alice.

"Then it doesn't matter which way you go," said the Cat.

"—so long as I get somewhere," Alice added as an explanation.

"Oh, you're sure to do that," said the Cat,
"if you only walk long enough."

—From *Alice in Wonderland* by Lewis Carroll

We all desire fun, fulfilling lives that are uniquely ours. Most of us don't want completely different lives than we have now, but we do want less stress and more options. In order to accomplish this—in order to make sh*t happen—you need a sense of the current landscape. How else will you know what to do differently?

Awareness of this landscape—the first of the Four Stages of Making Sh*t Happen—will prove to be both entertaining *and* painfully revealing. Very few people dare to venture as far as they can into the depths of awareness. The side effects of this fear manifest themselves as job burnout, uninspired living, perpetual tiredness, lack of motivation, fear and uncertainty, and general apathy. I can tell you, however, that becoming more aware will cultivate knowledge and understanding, so that you may enjoy and appreciate the world around you and put yourself miles ahead of your peers.

Awareness takes an inventory of everything that is and was. When you realize where you currently are and how you got there, you then have the knowledge to choose what you want to do—more of the same, or something different? Remember Alice and the Cat? If you don't know where you want to go, then you won't be able to take the appropriate actions to get there. Awareness is about figuring that out.

Awareness is *not* judging and picking yourself apart. It is the opposite of deconstructing. It is constructing your life from the challenges, fears, desires, habits, talents, strengths, and opportunities you have.

The beauty of becoming well versed in all things concerning you is that you are training yourself to be open and honest in life. You are learning to see things for how they really are, before determining how you want them to be or wish they were. You'll begin to see that you are in control of your own choices, your own actions, and even your own reactions.

So *how* do you go about creating awareness in your own life? First you ask yourself powerful questions; then you observe and interpret the answers, feelings, and reactions that ensue. During the awareness process you are always drawing conclusions about your behaviors, thoughts, and patterns. Let me be very clear: Awareness is *not* judging and picking yourself apart. It is the opposite of deconstructing. It is constructing your life from the challenges, fears, desires, habits, talents, strengths, and opportunities you have, a process that begins with an examination of both the scripts buried in your unconscious and the feelings and gut reactions you experience every day.

CONSCIOUS VS. UNCONSCIOUS

Our unconscious never forgets anything. Scientists have found that all of our life experiences cause physical changes in our brains. This means that our minds are literally shaped by our past. Your unconscious, the part of you that runs on autopilot, is like a vinyl record—imprinted with your past experiences, your habits, and the environments you place yourself in—that spins its tune over and over again in your life. It is important to listen closely to this "tune" and begin to understand its rhythm and melody.

On the other hand, our conscious mind only has control of about two to four percent of our functions and actions. This part of the mind is where we experience life on a daily basis. Think of your conscious mind as the gatekeeper, watching and filtering most—but not all—experiences that you have before giving them to your unconscious for processing and storage. Think of your unconscious mind as the doer, the part of you that stores your entire past and directs your conscious mind to pursue actions that produce the most desired results for you.

The best part is, a lot of our unconscious is built on what *we think and tell ourselves* every day—we have the power to change the inputs.

But in order to change negative thoughts and behaviors—and thus reset attitudes and beliefs in a way that helps us—we must first become more aware of what they are to begin with. This means watching how we interact with others and listening to what we tell ourselves. If it turns out that we're not happy with what we're seeing and hearing, then it's time to start arguing, rebutting, and disagreeing with ourselves.

> # When you pay attention to what you are feeling about people and circumstances, your motivations become clear.

For example, if you are having a cup of coffee with a friend and find yourself preoccupied with thoughts about how you are being perceived (*Do I sound smart? Is my hair okay?*) or worries about what might happen (*Will I run into my old boyfriend?* or (*I hope nobody sees me here.*), it's time to reevaluate what you're choosing to think about. What if instead you could be calm, present, fully engaged, and able to sit with a boss, colleague, or friend and see the whole picture without getting caught up in your own mind or feeling self-conscious? It's possible with greater awareness of what your conscious mind is feeding your unconscious.

LEARN TO FEEL

Long before I got in touch with my own emotions, I would joke with a friend of mine by saying, "Feelings are stupid!" In reality, feelings are extremely important, of course—why else would the English language have around four thousand words for them?

Feelings are excellent message receptors and senders that give us crucial information about our internal and external environments. When you pay attention to what you are feeling about people and circumstances, your motivations become clear. You may discover that your feelings are misguided and are not necessarily based in reality. They could stem from an incorrect belief that you have been carrying around with you for many years.

If you find yourself very frustrated, overwhelmed, or disoriented, stop and ask yourself, *Why am I feeling like this right now?* The truth is that we all project our own perspectives onto the facts of a situation; we all have our default emotional states we use to interpret information. Too often we have a predisposition to generate negative feelings based on misunderstandings of a situation.

THINKING WITH A PEN

The best way to start creating awareness is to take an inventory of these thoughts and emotions. Find or buy yourself a journal or notebook and write in it often. It's yours: You can write whatever you want, whenever you want. (But remember it's always best to ask your-self positive, actionable, high-quality questions so that you can get matching answers.)

HELPFUL TIPS

Keep the following points in mind as you work through the upcoming material, and if you ever feel lost, refer to them to help guide you in the right direction.

- Be clear and specific.
- Ask better questions to get better answers.
- Where your attention goes, energy flows.
- You get what you are looking for.
- Committed vs. interested:
  - Interested means you do what is convenient.
  - Committed means you do whatever it takes.
- Insanity = doing the same thing over and over and expecting a different result.
- Ask yourself, *Is this my best?*
- Forward progress is success.
- Measure often.

Most important tip:
- Don't feel overwhelmed. I'm going to help you through this process!

Sometimes the habit of writing can be tough to get into, but the process of writing is essential to understanding what is really going on between your ears, in your body, and in the world around you. Once you've written it all down—and, in effect, made it tangible—you will be able to decide if you want to keep thinking those thoughts or if you want to think something different. I have compiled a list of writing topics below to get you started. They will help you uncover the thoughts that rattle around inside your head and will help you begin flipping over the puzzle pieces of your life. You will need to set time aside to reflect on these questions and ideas so you can provide yourself with honest feedback. Take a few days, or weeks, to get through them. Write the answers out one at a time. Try not to avoid any questions. Come back to your answers and see if you can add anything else to them. Add your own questions to the list. This is just for you, so be as honest and open as you can.

What are your fears?
Only by exploring your fears will you be able to label them clearly, look at them more objectively, and dissect them one by one. Afterward you can make new choices around them and take different actions that will help you overcome and eliminate them.

- What emotions, ideas, situations, thoughts, or scenarios worry you day to day?
- What do you do to avoid these fears?
- What good has come from avoiding them?
- What have you missed out on because of them?
- Why do you want to be free of them now?

What do you currently focus on?
What you focus on shapes your entire world. Understanding this focus will give you insight on what's happening in your day-to-day

life, an awareness that leads to change.

- What are the subjects and ideas you think about and discuss during your daily conversations? What feelings occur during these conversations?
- What are your most common thoughts, worries, joys, and pleasures throughout the day?
- What emotions do you experience throughout the day? *Make both a positive and negative list.*
- What is your daily routine from waking up to going to sleep?
- What do you *want* to focus on every day?
- How much of your daily focus is spent on the positive and how much is spent on the negative?

Conduct a personal SWOT analysis

A SWOT analysis is a strategic balance sheet of an organization—a summary of its *strengths* and *weaknesses* and of the *opportunities* and *threats* it's facing. It is one of the key analytical tools to help an organization better understand itself, the competition, and the marketplace. We can perform this same analysis to better understand ourselves as individuals and to see things from a new perspective. The awareness we gain of our external and internal contexts helps us develop a vision and a strategy that link the two. Explore the following:

- your strengths
- your weaknesses
- your opportunities
- your threats

Take a general inventory of your life

A story is an account of real and imaginary events that make up a narrative. We each have stories, which are the narratives of our lives. We tell this story to others and ourselves every moment of the day. Right now you might not be telling the best, most accurate version of your story. By taking an inventory of your life events, you can uncover the facts of your story and piece together a better narrative that tells your story in a more inspiring, more enjoyable manner.

- What are your various personal achievements?
- What kinds of interesting or unique skills or abilities do you have?
- What setbacks or challenges have you encountered in your life?
- What are the major milestones and victories you've reached?

What are your current beliefs, opinions, and ideas about the "big issues"—money, love, success, and more? What is your relationship with them?

Our beliefs are shaped by everything from our environment to our genetics, but if you want to change a particular area of your life, you must first be clear about what your beliefs are in regard to that area. Start by examining your relationship with each category below and write down your current beliefs, opinions, and ideas about each of them.

- money
- love
- success
- happiness
- career
- health
- life
- goals
- risk
- faith
- exercise
- time
- family
- friends
- where you live
- your country
- the world

BUILDING YOUR IDENTITY

Do you like the identity you've created for yourself? If not, then it's on you to create the one you want. Maybe you choose to be somebody who is on top of things and doesn't procrastinate, or someone who listens before speaking. Maybe you choose to be someone who smiles a lot, or is charismatic. Maybe you choose to be a great wife, mother, sister, aunt, or daughter. Whatever it is, in order to change, you must begin acting on it right now.

When you actively choose your identity, you define the set of rules you want to live by. If you choose to be somebody who listens rather than gets defensive when confronted with a challenge, then when a challenge arises you can act based on the new identity you have chosen for yourself and not just default to the identity that's gotten you exactly where you are right now. If you don't know what your current identity is, ask some of the people around you. You can decide if you want to embody the identity others perceive you as having, or if you want to be somebody different. Every day you get the opportunity to live your identity. If you come up short on it, learn to do better next time. Then practice, practice, practice your chosen identity and watch your life transform.

TAKE IMMEDIATE ACTION

The quality of our lives is directly proportionate to the effort we put forth. If you are simply sitting on your sofa, cruising through these ideas on happiness and how to make changes hoping that they will magically work, you are mistaken. You need to take new actions to get new results. Pull out a piece of paper and get started on the Thinking With a Pen list right now before you keep reading. These kinds of small actions are the difference between where you are and where you want to be.

Pick three words that describe the identity you wish to embody and write them down in your notebook right now. Then dig deeper: Compile everything from who you are to who you want to be, so that you can build a list and foundation that you can always refer to and build upon.

ADVICE IN THE MIRROR

We are really good at giving advice to others. It is taking that great advice we share with them and using it ourselves that is tough. Use this exercise to give advice to those around you, and then turn it around and see which pieces of that advice you can apply to yourself. In order for this to work, you must be honest, specific, and direct with the advice you have for those around you.

Start by asking, *Who is frustrating me? Who would I like to give a piece of my mind to?* Write down his or her name and the advice you have for this person about how he or she should act differently. Write it as precisely as you can, whether that takes two words or five pages.

Example: Mom, stop criticizing me about the same things all the time and stop being afraid that I won't take care of myself, or that my job isn't good enough, because I'm an adult and I can take care of myself just fine!

....

....

....

Now, replace this person's name with your own name and rewrite the advice to yourself. Read this advice back to yourself, because it also applies to you.

....

....

....

....

PERMISSION SLIPS

The person that's already doing the thing they are seeking is so much more desirable—professionally, romantically, socially—than the person waiting for someone else to give them the opportunity to do it. Are you currently wrestling with a change in habit or belief that could move you forward, but you're too shy or afraid to deal with it right now? Complete the permission slip below to grant yourself permission to face it head-on. Pin the completed slip somewhere you will see it every day so that it will be a constant reminder that you have permission to do what you want. You don't have to wait until the market changes, or the climate improves, or the timing is just right. You can create awareness in your life by giving yourself permission to tap into what you truly desire *right now*. Do this with anything you want but feel you're denying yourself. Understand what you want by creating awareness, and then give yourself permission to have it. Now, take action. Use permission slips as often as you like. Here are some examples:

- I give James permission to not be fearful and to say yes whenever he wants.
- I give James permission to be happy.
- I give James permission to let go of his last relationship and move forward in order to find someone new who makes him smile and brings excitement to his life.
- I give James permission to let go of the resentment and forgive his parents for getting divorced.

Date: ....

I give permission to: ....

....

For the purpose of: ....

....

Authorize to grant permission (sign here): ....

WRAPPING UP AWARENESS

As you move out of the awareness stage and give yourself permission to pursue your desires, your focus will start to shift to applying and practicing what you have learned about your beliefs, attitudes, emotions, and behaviors. Now that you've got a clearer picture of what truly exists, you will start to feel more comfortable with yourself and those around you. You will begin to feel grounded and excited about making changes in your life. You will feel that the things you want to achieve are really not as difficult as you once thought.

> **When you actively choose your identity, you define the set of rules you want to live by.**

Now that you are aware that you possess the information you need to make creative choices, I'm going to prove to you what a critical role choice plays in your life. I'd like to start by showing you how to make the most effective choices to get exactly what you want in this world.

STAGE TWO
Choice

"With great power comes great responsibility." This is a quote from the French philosopher Voltaire, but most of us know it from the Spider-Man movie. We have the responsibility to carve out the lives we want by harnessing the massive power of choice.

I like to think of choice as a series of paths. From the moment you are born, there are millions and millions of tiny pathways that are all scrambled together and interlinked and running in the background of your life. As you begin to grow up, you start to walk down some of these paths. The list of choices you are faced with is truly unending. Perhaps you choose to hang out with the kids in drama classes, do extra-credit assignments, date an older person, go to summer camps, be mean to your friends, marry your high school sweetheart, or move to another state. Each time you make a choice, or someone else makes a choice for you, pathways disappear and new ones open up.

Throughout our lives we are constantly choosing which pathways to take. These choices merge and lead us to a destination that some like to call destiny. The power of choice is so fundamental to grasp because it holds the keys to being happy with the shape of your life. Perhaps you're evaluating the choices you have made thus far and you don't like what you are seeing, or maybe you don't really remember the choices you have made but you are unhappy with your current circumstances. I'm here to tell you that choice is so beautiful, and so powerful, that even if you feel like you've landed at the wrong destination, you can still forge into uncharted territory and find new paths to take. No matter where you are right now, you can create a life that you want and deserve.

FEARING CHOICE

Most of us in North America and other developed regions of the world live immensely privileged lives. When we go grocery shopping, we have thousands of food products to choose from—processed, unprocessed, dark chocolate, no chocolate, oats, grain, barley, rice, white bread, rye bread, whole-wheat bread, twelve-grain bread, six-grain bread, pumpernickel bread, soy bread, sourdough bread, French bread . . . The list goes on and on. The problem with all these choices is that we become paralyzed—and less satisfied when we do finally make a choice. More choice does not equal more happiness; in fact it typically means less. We tend to become frustrated and fearful of making the wrong decisions rather than excited at the ability to have choice. Adding options equals less satisfaction when we do finally choose, because we are constantly debating whether or not we made the right choice.

Plus, it's a lot of work having to sift through millions of options that are thrown our way on a daily basis. Having to make so many choices also causes us to develop extremely high expectations that are very rarely met. This can leave us with an underlying sense of dissatisfaction. This "choice paradox" is the peculiar problem of all modern, affluent societies. Now don't get me wrong—it's wonderful that we have so many choices! The problem is that most of us were not taught how to choose. We stand at a crowded buffet table of choice, paralyzed by the fear that with so much to choose from, we might make the wrong decision.

INTUITION AND LEARNING TO CHOOSE

In his book *Blink*, Malcolm Gladwell discusses an experiment performed by a team of scientists at the University of Iowa. The experiment involved a group of gamblers and two decks of rigged cards. The scientists hooked each gambler up to a machine that measured the activity of the sweat glands in the palms of their hands. The study found that the gamblers started generating stress responses to the red decks (the less favorable deck) by the tenth card, forty cards before they were able to say that they had a hunch about what was wrong with the two decks. The part of our brain that leaps to conclusions like this is called the "adaptive unconscious." Studies like this University of Iowa one have opened up new fields in the realm of psychology: Underneath our conscious awareness, our minds are operating on a strategy that knows a lot more than we think we know.

> **When you learn to develop and trust your instincts and let your intuition guide your decision-making processes, you will find that the quality of your choices improves exponentially.**

Everyone has heard the phrases "Follow your instincts" and "My gut just told me that something was wrong." These phrases illustrate the intuition that all human beings possess. Your intuition is essentially your gut instinct—and your gut instinct can, perhaps paradoxically, be trained, as we explored earlier. These gamblers exhibited stress responses precisely because they'd played cards for years—they'd "trained" their unconscious to look for certain patterns and deviations from patterns. This "training" of instinct takes practice, persistence, and patience.

To reprogram this decision-making center of your brain, you need to consult your core emotional center *before* you consult your conscious mind. In the rigged card-player experiment, the players knew deep down that something was wrong, yet they kept consciously making the choices, which *appeared* to be correct at the time. When you learn to develop and trust your instincts and let your intuition guide your decision-making processes, you will find that the quality of your choices improves exponentially.

In any case, remember your limitations regarding control. Stephen Covey's 90/10 principle states that 90 percent of life is in your control, but you cannot control the other 10 percent. For example, you cannot control a driver cutting you off in traffic, or your flight being late, or your coffee being knocked over by a random stranger. What you can control, however, is how you react. Your reactions are what make up 90 percent of the results you are seeing in your life today. If someone cuts you off in traffic, you can curse and honk and work yourself up into a frenzy of anger, or you can choose to take an annoyed deep breath and let it roll off your back because, hey, there are bigger things in the day to spend your energy on.

AVOIDING WHAT YOU DON'T WANT

What we think manifests in our lives. Our unconscious brain will take our thoughts, regardless of whether they are good or bad, and translate them into instructions. When your conscious brain says "I hate my job," over and over, your unconscious brain reads this as an instruction, and these instructions become the driving force behind the actions that you inevitably take. In turn, the negative instructions that you have given yourself become self-fulfilling prophecies. Owning your sh*t is not about avoiding or changing your situation, or even necessarily about changing any part of your life. It is about creating and focusing on the results that you want to see unfold around you. When you choose to focus on what you do want, you will find yourself taking actions that will inevitably create the circumstances and results that you want to see develop and unfold in your life.

THE POWER IN CHOICE

Power is the key sliding scale when it comes to choice. Where you believe the power is located in a situation affects the eventual choice you will make. If you think of the power within a situation as outside of yourself, you are leaving yourself at the mercy of that situation. This happens when you make choices based on consensus, elimination, default, reaction, or limitations. On the other hand, when you are focused on creating something you want, you will recognize that you have the power within you to eventually get it.

At any given moment, there is always a choice that you have power over. When you understand that you hold 90 percent of the power in your life, you will be able to make the best choices for yourself and create whatever you want in your life. Making this "power shift" will ease the paralysis of fear and hesitation. You won't feel regret or uncertainty in making any choice, because you will know that you always have the power, at any time, to simply make a new choice and create any new focus or result.

THE TWO TYPES OF CHOICES

Empowering, creative choices can mostly be categorized in two ways:

living choices and *doing* choices. You already know that creating awareness in your life involves dissecting your past choices, actions, and thoughts, and choosing to change your outcomes in the future by making better, more congruent choices. Let's explore how you can use the two choice categories to make more powerful and decisive choices in your life.

Living Choices

"Living choices" are what I call your foundation. These types of choices are about committing yourself to a specific way of living or being. A living choice is not a choice you make to "get you somewhere" or to move you forward in any particular direction. It's a choice in which you commit yourself to a basic life orientation or state of being. Some examples include living a healthy lifestyle or being a positive, happy person. Living choices are proactive. They use all the will and energy of the universe to align the necessary pieces to create the life that you want. Making strong living choices is the critical difference between being the creator of your own life and always feeling like you have fallen short. If you do not make good living choices, you will find yourself constantly searching for ways to alter your circumstances. Thinking the grass is greener on the other side of the fence is futile, and it's even worse to get a sore ass and no results from sitting on the fence all the time.

> **Making strong living choices is the critical difference between being the creator of your own life and always feeling like you have fallen short.**

Living choices won't be affected much by your external world. Living choices are the point in your life from which everything operates. Convenience, comfort, peer pressure, guilt, fear, pleasure—all of these stop being excuses once you have made a true living choice. For example, when you choose to be true to yourself no matter what, you are making a living choice.

If you find yourself wavering, looking for exceptions, or feeling unfulfilled, you probably have not made a living choice at all, but rather a circumstantial or situational choice. Once you make a living choice, a whole new understanding and state of being opens up, and reality takes on a clear, empowering tone.

Once you have made a choice to live in a particular, fundamental way, you may notice that you have many unwanted habits, behaviors, and thinking patterns. These will quickly disappear because they simply won't have anything to feed off of anymore. For example, if you choose to have a healthy mind, body, and soul, then you'll begin to attract everything that you define to be healthy for you, and those things that do not promote this orientation will fade away. Unhealthy options will still exist but won't be of interest or concern to you. Your thoughts will now be focused on an entirely new mandate. Living choices are about choosing to be your authentic self at a high level. Living choices are the major decisions of our lives that we only make a few times. So make good, solid living choices that are authentic to you.

Here are some examples of living choices:
- to have a healthy body, mind, and soul
- to have a life of my choosing
- to be the guiding force in my own life
- to live life on my terms
- to be of clear mind
- to be true to myself

Doing Choices

"Doing choices" are about creating results and making sh*t happen day to day. They are choices that have tangible and measurable results. These are choices that are whole unto themselves and feed the bigger living choices, and their primary function is to create a specific, immediate result, not start a process. They are not designed to lead you to something else—they are about creating results in a specific area.

Here are some examples of doing choices:
- playing the guitar because you value having a creative outlet and are passionate about music
- cooking because you love creating exquisite dishes
- flossing your teeth
- starting a business
- having a meaningful relationship or moving to a new country

You don't have to make a living choice in order to make good doing choices. You can create awesome results in many areas, but the long-term success of those results, if you wish to build on them, will require a living choice or else your life will eventually swing back to what you were doing before. If you find that you are not making choices on a daily basis that support what you truly want, then go back and examine what you believe: What fundamental living choices have you made in your life?

I CHOOSE...

Take out your notebook or journal. Using what you've learned about yourself in the awareness stage, create a clear, actionable vision of what you want and formally choose it. You must write it down and

say it out loud to yourself using the words, "*I choose* _____."
These words activate the power of choice and solidify your decision,
making it official. In order to create change or produce a new result,
you have to powerfully choose it. Perhaps your choice is "I choose
to pursue my dream of painting and I am moving to New York in
the new year." Or "I choose to wake up at six a.m. each weekday and
either run or go to the gym for forty-five minutes." Without the
words, the power is outside yourself and you have not claimed it.

The choices you have made will always reflect back to you in the
results you see around you. You get to choose your reality, whether
it is happiness or sadness, health or weakness, confidence or anxiety,
success or failure. The choice is always yours. As the late computer
scientist Randy Pausch so fondly said in his famous last lecture, "The
brick walls in life exist to keep those out who are not really serious
about getting what they want." Choosing is about breaking down
those walls.

WRAPPING UP CHOICE

Indecisiveness is a true killer of success and happiness. The most
successful people have the ability to make quick, accurate, powerful
decisions and to keep momentum up and the morale moving forward.
They have learned that if they can limit their options, they will
invariably make better choices and feel more satisfied with the final
results of their choice.

You activate the laws of the universe when you formally make
a choice. Once a choice is made, your brain is free to start focusing
on how to make your choice a reality, or how to put your choice into
action. The more you practice making choices, the better you get at
it. You will eventually learn to make the best choices that lead you
to even better results. Remember the example of the card players?
What that study proves is that you already know what to do. Develop

and use your gut instinct to make choices. When you operate from your gut, you move quickly and invariably make better choices. Bring a sense of urgency to what you want to accomplish and watch the power of your unconscious go to work as it nudges you toward making the most effective choices on a daily basis.

STAGE THREE
Action

Do you employ the if/then model of doing? *If* this one thing happens, you might tell yourself, *then* I will do that other thing. If a new job comes up, then I will leave the one I am currently doing and not enjoying. If I have a date, then I will decide to have fun this weekend. Or are you someone who has lots of good ideas but never acts on them? Maybe it's about getting a new job, starting a business, finding a new relationship, building a website, making a documentary—the list goes on.

If so, you're likely stuck in a *seeking* mindset rather than a *doing* one. In other words, your reality rests in the realm of the hypothetical instead of the experiential. When we put our ideas out there but don't act on them, our power to create loses momentum, and we stop taking our ideas and ourselves seriously. We risk losing credibility when we get known as a talker and not a doer. Do you want to be the kind of person who relives life through stories of great ideas that could have been but never materialized? The power to act is solely within you, and you don't have to rely on happenstance or on someone handing you an opportunity before you can start. You can create the momentum and results you are seeking. You are in control of making sh*t happen.

Let's say you're looking for a job as a web developer. Let's flip the tables and put you in the employer's or client's shoes. Consider who would be the most appealing person to hire—the person who's out there looking for a job as a web developer by sending out resumes and waiting for someone to offer them a job, or the person who's actively building websites of their own, creating tutorial videos, blogging, talking with others about web development, and going to events related to web development?

The same thing applies when you're looking for a new relationship. If you want to be with somebody who is active, outdoorsy, and enjoys photography, sailing, or rock climbing, then you need to go do those things now and often! Do the activities you want regardless. It's more likely that you'll connect with a partner who likes the things you like when you're actually out there doing those things. Remember: People are more attracted to a person who's in action rather than just waiting to be invited. At a party, who usually gets asked to dance: the wallflower, or the person smiling, dancing, and meeting new people? You can increase your odds of meeting a compatible partner, finding a new job, or making new friends if you are having fun and being the person doing, not seeking, what you want.

The biggest obstacle to action is focusing solely on the past. Many lament the fact that they can never get back a good thing they once had, like physical shape, love, or a higher-paying job. These kinds of thoughts get us nowhere. Stop collecting ideas about things that you could or should have done. Instead, go out and actually go *do these things*. Maybe you'll love it or maybe you'll hate it, but you'll have had a valuable experience either way and you will have gained credibility with yourself and those around you.

At the end of the day, the tales of great ideas gone nowhere are not the ones that captivate us. What are memorable are the stories of real experiences of success and failure. The errors, adventures, loves, losses, and laughter we experience from playing with life are the narrative nuts and bolts for great stories. Imagine the biography of a person who had nothing but ideas they never got around to pursuing. It would be the most boring book in the bookstore and no one would ever read it.

This chapter will help you become the person *doing*, not merely seeking or dreaming. It will show you how to take action and define what the properties, habits, and ideas are behind this *doing* part in the Four Stages of Making Sh*t Happen process. I will provide you with some solid how-to road map steps and ideas throughout this chapter to keep you on the course to your desired destination.

The awareness you gained in stage one has allowed you to clearly see where you are, and the choices you made in stage two have helped you decide where you want to go. In stage three, you will bring it all together with a plan, a road map that will start with the end result and work backward, charting all the steps right back to where you are now. Once you have broken down the steps, you simply live it forward. Things will change along the way, but you will have an idea of what you're in for and be well prepared.

As you move forward, remember to be patient. Even diamonds need long periods of constant pressure to form. Anything worth being, having, or creating in life will not be handed to you, nor will it show up when you expect it. Right now you're simply a diamond in the rough, and I'm going to teach you how to *extract* the best parts of yourself and leave the rest behind.

CLEAN UP THE CLUTTER AND TIE UP THE LOOSE ENDS

You can't just squish something new into your life; you've got to create the space for it. We have baggage, clutter, and a mess of loose ends blocking the way of the changes we want to occur. Often the clutter is not directly related to what we're trying to achieve, so it can be necessary to clean up our lives in all areas so the energy and opportunities we want can flow more freely. If you have a closet filled with clothes you haven't worn in years, then give them to charity or to a friend. If you've been putting off having an important discussion with someone, talk to him or her.

Take out a pen. I want you to make a list of all the things you are putting up with. You'll feel lighter when you get rid of all the unnecessary crap. Each time you clear out a new corner of your life, make sure you pause and enjoy the new empty space you've created. You may even choose to leave it empty. Remember, less is often more. If you do choose to fill up the vacant space, only fill it with things that you really want and appreciate—not just more "stuff." Once you have made a complete list of all the things weighing you down, build an action plan around cleaning up the clutter, tying up loose ends, and ending things you are putting up with—and then act!

Example cleaning list:
- Go through storage locker and donate things I will probably never use.
- Call Dad to apologize for car incident.
- Cancel membership to gym I never go to and sign up for dance classes instead.
- Finish writing book I started three years ago.
- Go through dishes and throw away chipped ones.

Example action plan:
I will spend Saturday, November 27 from 11 a.m. to 3 p.m. going through my closet and removing any clothes I haven't worn in over two years, and at 3 p.m. I will drive to St. Joseph's Church on Yew Street and donate my clothes.

Your cleaning list:

Your action plan:

BUILDING A PRIORITY LIST

We all have a hierarchy of things that we value or want in our lives, but often we're a little fuzzy on our priorities. Perhaps you're committed to Sunday dinners, going to the gym four times a week, having an active social life on the weekends, and a soccer practice once a week. All these things sit on a priority list.

We get frustrated when we think we value something highly but don't prioritize our time and resources for it. Maybe you think that creating a new business is your top priority, but in reality you spend more time thinking about and pursuing a new relationship. A situation like this can cause frustration, and constantly send you in circles chasing the business but not getting where you want with it. You may realize that the relationship is actually more important to you than the business because that is what you are actually putting first. Our actual priority is often what we automatically put first. If honest reflection shows you that the business really is your top priority right now, then you need to make your reality reflect that by spending more energy on the business. The result you seek will then be able to follow.

Your life flows when you have proper prioritization. You can't do everything at once! Your time, energy, effort, focus, money, attention—all your human resources—should go to your top priority. By taking care of your top priority, you will also feed your lower priorities. Be honest about what's at the top of your list. You are likely not being truthful when the stuff you are doing and spending your resources on are not at the top of your list. Be committed to making the stuff at the top happen. Less is more. Spend your resources wisely. Once we master the things at the top, we can move other things up the list, or even add new items, to keep life flowing. Priority lists evolve. Your task right now is to create an honest priority list for your life in this moment; then you'll follow it with an exercise that will help you figure out how to take the first steps to accomplish those priorities.

7–10 current goals, listed in priority:

1. ....
2. ....
3. ....
4. ....
5. ....
6. ....
7. ....
8. ....
9. ....
10. ....

Now, how to work through those priorites? That's where the next exercise comes in. It's about brainstorming multiple solutions to a problem, becoming aware of a variety of roads—or "entry points"— you could take to reach a result, and considering different people's perspectives along the way. Let's start with examples, and then you can begin writing your own entry points to things you are working on and start finding new ways to get to your result.

Examples:

A problem I have is: I need to get in shape.

- Entry Point 1: Join a boot camp class.
- Entry Point 2: Eat more veggies and less sugar.
- Entry Point 3: Run five days a week for thirty minutes.

A goal I have is: to create a successful wellness business.

- Entry Point 1: Learn and implement new business skills.
- Entry Point 2: Use my public relations skills to gain media coverage.
- Entry Point 3: Interview successful business owners for ideas and advice.

Now it's your turn . . .

A problem/goal/perspective I have is: ....

....

....

....

....

Entry Point 1: ....

....

....

Entry Point 2: ....

....

....

Entry Point 3: ....

....

....

ROUTINE BUILDING

When we have a good routine, we are able to do what we need to do to make the day feel like it is ours. At the end of any given day, if you have met your own expectations, you can go to sleep happy and free of worry. Maybe you count yourself among those people who don't like routines. Maybe you prefer a spontaneous life free of plans. If so, I want you to consider that it's not so much the routine that you dislike but the pattern of the routine. Everything in life has a pattern and path of least resistance, and even though you might prefer "spontaneity," there *is* a pattern and routine in the supposed randomness, which quietly provides the foundation for the thrills, creativity, and success that you are having in your life now. If there is less of this than you want at the moment, then building a better routine is the key to success, and not the enemy.

> Routines are ... about finding the *best result* with the minimum output at the *optimum moment.*

One important part of my routine is writing, but it has taken a while to find where it best fits into my life. When I tried writing in the morning, I found that my focus was disrupted by the tasks I needed to accomplish that day. Plus, I'm not an early-morning person. When I tried writing in the afternoon, I always wanted to run errands, walk my dog, and work with clients. For me, writing requires a long stretch of uninterrupted creative hours, so the afternoon was no good. I found my fit, you've probably guessed, writing late at night. At this time of day, nothing is needed of me. When I sit down to write at night, I've already accomplished all my tasks for the day, visited with everyone, walked the dog, ran, ate . . . and the world is quiet. After finding my own sweet spot, my writing flourished.

Routines are a finicky dance and aren't always perfect: It may seem impossible to assemble all the steps, but if you stay creative, and keep trying, you'll eventually piece it all together. It's about finding the *best result with the minimum output at the optimum moment.*

You already have a daily routine, but if you're like most people, you haven't given much thought to what it is and whether it's a good fit for you. Most of us have a fairly regular schedule with typical work hours, usual times we sleep and wake up, the time we go to the gym, the time we spend socializing, or specific days we do family activities. The awareness stage has helped you discover your current routines, put them under a microscope, and decide what's working and what's not. Consciously building your routine begins with looking at all the pieces of your daily life. What time do you get up? How long do you need for breakfast? Do you need to commute? Do you need to get the kids to school? Do you need to plan lunch? Do you have a meeting at three o'clock? Do you need to go for a run in the evening?

Great routines set you up for success by always allotting a realistic amount of time for each activity. It's important to book more time for something rather than less. For instance, allot one hour for something even if it can be done in thirty to forty-five minutes. With this scenario you will likely finish on time, if not early.. By constantly underestimating the amount of time needed to do things, you leave yourself feeling as if you're always behind. This angst weighs on us.

The basic elements of a successful day include sleeping well, eating well, exercising, creating a living, and having some free creative time and space for special things that make you feel fulfilled. Great routines are about connecting with people, giving, and helping or sharing with others. Maybe sitting for half an hour every morning with a cup of tea is what you need to feel like you, or maybe it's going for a morning run. When you decide what you want to do, put it down on paper; visualizing will help you realize what exactly it is you value enough to incorporate into your daily life. Good routines also make room for unstructured "blue sky" time. This free time encourages new people and ideas to enter your life, and it is where you will find creativity and inspiration. You can start by considering what you most value. What are the things you are spending your time on? Write down the things that you really love, value, and that make you feel like you:

....

....

....

....

....

Are you doing these things on a regular basis? Are you also taking the small daily steps to reach your big goals? Of the things you most value, write down which ones you're doing and which ones you're not:

I am doing . . . .

....

....

I am not doing . . . .

....

....

....

You now have the amazing opportunity to build a new routine that actually reflects your goals and values. Once you have written down your current routine, begin to add the elements that you want to

Start by considering what you most value.

have in your life and subtract the things you are currently doing but don't need or want to do. Start experimenting with the best times to work new things into your day, and revise your routine as required. Once you've reflected thoroughly on where you are and where you want to be, you can then make your routine razor sharp by using a daily task-management plan.

DAILY TASK-MANAGEMENT PLAN

If you want to build a daily routine that aligns with your values and allows you to live a life you love, then you'll need to start actively managing your daily priorities, tasks, and overall time.

At the end of each day, review and check off the progress of the top portion of a daily task-management form, and then take a moment to reflect upon the results and feedback of your day's efforts. Complete the top portion of it again for the next day. Once you have completed the top portion and have listed all the items and tasks you need to complete for tomorrow, open up whatever device you have for scheduling your day and schedule those must-do items. Be sure to allot generous amounts of time for each task so that you don't set yourself up for failure or frustration. Your day should not be completely full, but will now have a few items that you *must* and *need* to get done scheduled, so that when you start your day tomorrow you'll already have a plan and can begin without wasting time.

The "all other tasks" section of the daily task-management plan is very important. It's the place for you to record everything you need or want to do so that nothing is forgotten or pops up and derails your day. As things come up during the day, you can add them to this list, but make sure to not overwhelm yourself with things to be done. A daily task-management plan is there to help you focus on doing the important things each day, as well as to make sure you're aware of all of the tasks you face so you can make better use of your time. Here are the rules of a successful daily task-management plan:

Commitment: You must commit to this plan every day, or you will not see positive results. You cannot do it a little or every once in a while. Make daily task management a habit by doing it to the best of your ability every day.

Scheduling: Make sure that you complete the plan every day at the same time. It's ideal to write down tomorrow's tasks the night before while you have momentum and the ideas fresh in your mind. If it helps, set a reminder at the end of each day to work on your daily task-management planning.

72-Hour Rule: Nothing on your plan should stay there for more than seventy-two hours. That means if you put a task or item on your plan—even if it's in the "all other tasks" section—and you have not completed that item within seventy-two hours, it will now become a "top *must-do* priority" item for the next day. This will eliminate procrastination and force you to keep moving forward rather than getting stuck on certain tasks.

Day Timer: Make sure you don't just complete the plan at the end of each day but that you go the final step and put the tasks into your day timer, calendar, or phone so that they are scheduled and ready for you to execute.

Checking Items Off: Make sure to check items off throughout the day, or at the end of the day, so that you can see what you have completed and what's still left to do. This will give you a sense of accomplishment and progress.

Feedback: The only way to improve is to monitor your progress and pay attention to what works for you and what doesn't. If you find something is not meshing well for you, then tweak it until it works. Use the bottom portion of the plan to make daily notes so you can reflect each day. Be sure to note ways to improve your use of time and effort.

DAILY TASK-MANAGEMENT PLAN FORM

TOP *MUST-DO* PRIORITIES

These are the **top one to three** things that you *must* get done. **Schedule them** into your day timer so they have an appropriate time and duration to be worked on and completed. **They cannot be put off**, so make sure to do them before anything else.

Task	End-of-day status
1.	
2.	
3.	

CONTINUED ON NEXT PAGE

NEED TO GET DONE

These are the tasks that you need to get done after your top must-do priorities. Schedule these into your day timer where appropriate.

Task	End-of-day status
→	
→	
→	
→	

ALL OTHER TASKS

Anything that you need to do that is not a must-do or need-to-get-done task. These are big or small items and must be accounted for so they don't get forgotten about, but they are not necessarily urgent.

Task	End-of-day status
→	
→	
→	
→	

END-OF-DAY FEEDBACK

What was the result of the day? Positive, negative, challenging, filled with lessons, hopeful? List what worked, what didn't work, and what you can do differently to improve tomorrow and beyond:

Task	End-of-day status
→	
→	
→	
→	

FREEDOM SPOT

You've just developed a priority list, routine, and daily task-management plan, but focusing only on the tasks and goals can become very process driven. You must always stay connected to yourself. So as you're planning, don't forget to consider placing "freedom spots" into your day. A freedom spot is a moment in the day where you feel free. This is a moment you own, where everything else that's happening outside of the present fades away. Life is on your terms in that moment and there is nothing but bliss.

Our freedom spot is different for each of us. Maybe it's your morning coffee, the run you take at lunch, or enjoying an afternoon stroll with your dog while everyone else is working. Wherever it happens, your freedom spot is a reminder that life is sweet and blissful, and there are moments of it that shine with the ownership we have over our lives.

A great goal is to try to enjoy your freedom spot multiple times a day. It doesn't have to be long, but let it expand by fully immersing yourself in the experience. When you have a freedom spot to go to, no matter what is happening in your life, you will always have perspective and a centered frame of reference for each day.

OVERCOMING FEAR

Some types of fear are good. These kinds of fear act as survival mechanisms, warning us of danger and death. But most fear that we modern-day humans experience tends to set false limits. As a result we subject ourselves to situations that we don't want because we are afraid of standing up for ourselves, speaking our mind, and making choices. We don't like where we are, but we are too afraid to change it so we put up with it and hate ourselves and those around us. What kind of life is this?

Always remember this simple truth when you find yourself

fearful of an unknown outcome: It's never as bad as you think. If it is as bad as you think, there are outside factors contributing to it (the 10 percent you cannot control), and this is very rare.

But overcoming fear isn't about taking too big of an initial leap. We tend to do this when we have been held back by fear for too long and finally muster up the courage to leap. It is a blind, messy leap that simply justifies the fear. This makes us more stuck, not less.

No wonder we are afraid of failure; we haven't learned to pace ourselves and follow a simple, easy, strategic action plan. Remember that you don't have to achieve an end goal to feel success—you just need to make progress. What can you do right now to build momentum toward your goal and overcome your fear? Don't try and run a marathon six weeks from now if you've been inactive for ten years. Similarly, don't try and earn $1 million in one year if you've never worked for yourself and made over $60,000. Pace yourself and build into it. Dream big, but implement steady growth plans that are realistic and enjoyable. If you do this, you will feel successful throughout the whole process and you will overcome fear as you progress toward your desired outcome.

The worst-case scenario exercise is one way of overcoming the fear of the unknown and of failure. It helps you to confront your worst nightmares head-on. Let's say you hate your job and you think you'll get fired because you aren't performing well. The emotional resonance you would feel around this situation is probably far worse than the real-life "worst-case scenario" would merit. Consider the options you'd have if you got fired—facts only. Why would you get fired? What would that mean? Would you get a severance? Do you have another job lined up? Do you have money saved? Could you go live with friends or family?

The worst-case scenario exercise will help you put your worst-case fears into perspective and form a "just in case" plan. If you are about to get fired, for instance, you have at least two options (and I recommend you do both): Smarten up so you save your job, and start looking for another job you actually want to do. Remember, what we focus on becomes our reality. If you are focused on getting fired, it's much more likely to happen than if you are focused on doing your best or finding another job that better suits you. The reality is usually not nearly as extreme as we imagine it, yet we think and act as if our biggest fear is the only possible result. This exercise is about creating more options and making a plan for the worst so that anything less will be easier to handle. Sit down in a quiet place with your journal and work through the following questions:

What am I worried about?

Why am I worried about it?

What is the worst thing that could possibly happen as a result?

What are my options if the worst thing did happen?

What will most likely happen?

What actions can I take now to prepare myself?

What actions can I take now to correct the current situation?

WRAPPING UP ACTION

Your eye is more likely to see something that is moving versus standing still. It's the same with living your life—you learn as you live. If you only ever plan and replan, you're not going to see where your trouble or opportunity spots are. You've *got to jump in* and try out your plan. If it fails (and it will far more than it succeeds at the beginning) then you can readjust your plan and make it better. You figure out how to make it better as you go based on the feedback you get from doing something, regardless of success or failure.

You're not going to gain any valuable experience sitting on the sidelines dreaming and wishing. Making sh*t happen is not about attaining perfection; it's about taking action that will move you toward your desired outcome. Aiming for perfect will kill your momentum to act. "Good enough" is where most of us need to land, and then we can keep adjusting and moving forward from there. Babies learn to stand up and walk because they keep getting up after falling down. They learn what not to do so that they can maintain their center of gravity and keep putting one foot in front of the other. Your action plan, much like life, is organic and always changing, adjusting and evolving. Jump in and get started!

STAGE FOUR
Commitment

Commitment is the engine of making sh*t happen. Once you've chosen a path and have begun to move forward on it, commitment is what keeps you going.

Keeping that engine in tip-top shape isn't easy. Consistency and follow-through—which are at the heart of commitment—are challenging habits to adopt, especially when we've spent years complacent or apathetic. Much time, energy, resourcefulness, and vulnerability is required of us to make up for the ground we've lost, but only once we've prepared ourselves to do whatever is necessary—only once we're committed—will we be able to achieve the results we're seeking.

In this final stage, we'll touch on the mindsets and behaviors necessary for lasting commitment.

EMBRACING THE UNCOMFORTABLE

One of the most important lessons you can learn as you move toward creating the life you want is to *embrace* the uncomfortable.
This means you need to stop giving a shit about what people think.
It means you need to create awareness in your life about where you are now in relation to where you want to be. It means you need to

make the choice to own your sh*t and go after your heart's true desire—no matter what other people may think.

As you begin to own your sh*t and follow through on your commitments to yourself, you'll start to feel more secure. This will make it easier to embrace the uncomfortable moments. As you begin understanding yourself, your goals, and your circumstances better, you'll see fewer and fewer of these moments.

When anything—from a conversation to a relationship—gets uncomfortable, our first instinct is to stop or escape. We don't like to be uncomfortable because we never learned how to stick through it until the discomfort fades. We are taught to both pursue and value comfort and ease in our lives. This is a dangerous mindset. It neglects the idea that sometimes we need to travel through discomfort to get to higher ground. This is why so many relationships fail. It's hard to embrace the uncomfortable when the going gets tough, and when you don't see eye to eye with your partner, it's easier to leave or blame them than it is to embrace the uncomfortable and honestly evaluate the best way to proceed.

> **When you feel uncomfortable, you've hit a nerve of truth.**

The uncomfortable parts of life are where most of our learning happens. An atmosphere of growth is essential to happiness. We need to train ourselves not to run at the first sign of discomfort, but to instead question *why* we feel uncomfortable with a person, feeling, or a particular situation.

When you feel uncomfortable, you've hit a nerve of truth—it's your emotional center trying to tell you something about yourself. If you "feel into" the discomfort and stick it out by staying committed, you will stumble upon the breakthrough.

If I'd given up on running when I first started, I would have never been able to finish a half marathon. I would never have gotten to the place I'm at now, loving to run for the sake of just running. To get here, I had to hurt my body and endure endless shitty runs. I had to get off the sofa when it was raining and force myself out of my apartment. I embraced the uncomfortable parts of running because my commitment to it required me to push through the discomfort at the beginning.

PRACTICE

Professional athletes don't often get asked about all the time that they spend training. We prefer to watch and cheer them on as they race toward victory. We want the sound-bite success story, not the details of years of dedication and hard work. Once you are committed to achieving an outcome, you arrive at the hard part of long hours, pain, and sacrifice. The good news is that once you have succeeded in a certain area of your life, the process gets easier and easier. Practice really does make perfect. It's never as hard the second time around—wisdom only understood through experience.

The process of commitment and success must be discovered on your own. We're all afraid of this in-between time, and look for shortcuts to avoid the pains of this process. That's probably why you bought this book and other books and programs—you're looking for a way to have it all nicely laid out so it doesn't have to be hard. I'm probably not the first person to tell you that that's just not the way life works. Achieving anything in life requires long-term, committed practice.

TEST AND REFOCUS

Typically when our plans do not go the way we thought they would, we quit. We allow our setbacks to define us and to be the end result of our effort. Lack of faith in ourselves is the root cause of so much anxiety and disappointment. When it comes to committing all the way, we often feel anxious or doubtful about getting the results we want. For example, when learning to play guitar, we might accept the temporary feedback that it's hard or that we aren't rock gods in a month and quit too early. Staying committed to your end result means testing your road map. If feedback indicates that your current approach is not working, you need to refocus. We quit and fall off the wagon because we take feedback too personally and define ourselves by it. Understand that the feedback is really about our action plans or road maps, not our capacity or worth. Negative feedback is temporary, and it's our job to refocus and try a new approach until we get the result we desire.

When you are truly committed, you won't quit when your first, second, or even third approach doesn't go the way you had hoped. If you treat life this way, as a series of tests and lessons, you will refocus and retest until you find an approach that works for you.

THE GAME OF SUCCESS, HAPPINESS, AND ACHIEVEMENT
Ask any successful or happy person and they will tell you that once you've succeeded or been happy for long enough, the whole process becomes a game you enjoy playing. That's because the muscles in your body literally store records of the activities you perform in muscle memory, and the same can be said of your body's experience with happiness.

Commitment is not all work and no play. Staying committed to developing new habits and patterns of success and happiness lends itself to creating a new point of reference that your mind and body can build from. If you've already achieved something, you can leverage the past victory to fuel your future endeavors. Happy, successful people understand this principle, and that is why they are not attached to every positive or negative outcome to everything that happens in their lives. They have seen and done enough to know that you win some and you lose some.

Life is not necessarily about the end result—it's about the journey. Not being attached and not being committed are two very different things, and it is important that you do not confuse them. You can be committed to a result such as learning to drive, but you can be unattached to the process. Perhaps you fail your first driving test, so you decide to approach your driving lessons differently and hire a private instructor. You are committed to the outcome of receiving your license, but are unattached to the result of failing the first time. You simply try again and readjust your road map until you get what you want.

WRAPPING UP COMMITMENT

Commitment takes *patience*. Time is an underestimated piece of the puzzle. If you have gone through the stages so far—created awareness, made your choices, and built a plan of action with strong *why* reasons—then you will find it easier to stay focused and patient as you work toward making sh*t happen. When your patience and focus start to dwindle because you've hit a temporary wall, you must remember that just because you want something now doesn't mean that it will show up now. Remember, making sh*t happen is an investment. If you don't stay focused and patient, what you want will never show up, ever, and you won't end up where you want to be.

Having patience as you work toward your goals will determine just how fast you achieve your desired outcome and how far you'll go. We live in a world where everything seems to happen so quickly and easily, but the things we really want to manifest don't work that way. Write down the following personal declaration of commitment to the process and stick it on your wall, mirror, fridge, car, or anywhere you can easily remind yourself to step up and be committed!

PERSONAL DECLARATION OF COMMITMENT

I, _____ , commit to FULLY owning
my sh*t—including all the good, bad, ugly, unknown, and indifferent
pieces of my life. It's my life and up to me to make it awesome.
I will let go of who I think I should be so I can free who I am.
I am committed to making the things I want in this life happen.
I will focus on being better rather than being right or wrong.

WRAPPING UP THE FOUR STAGES

As you follow the Four Stages of Making Sh*t Happen, you will
find that your personal energy is king. Energy is what drives you
on toward your desired outcome. It's the fuel that allows your
creativity to flow. But every day there will be distractions from the
actions necessary to toward your outcome.

Your time and energy are the most valuable resources that you
own because once they are spent, you cannot get them back. When
you waste your energy, you lose the real value of your life, and when
you actually want to make sh*t happen, the energy won't be there.
Don't just give your time away freely or spend it frivolously on
anyone or anything that bids for it; if you do, you will ultimately lose
patience with your dreams, your goals, and yourself. Think about
what you spend each minute of your day on and where you allow
your energy to go. Whom and what do you give most of your energy
to?

All of us, from time to time, need an energy recharge so we can
keep going and stay committed. When you find your energy waning
and you need some more of it as soon as possible, use these favorite
tips of mine to help you push through to the end:

Stand up, stretch, and take a couple of deep breaths
Stretch your arms, back, legs, and neck. Take a deep breath through your nose, hold it, and let it out slowly and forcefully. Repeat several times. When you sit back down, you'll have the clear head and fresh feeling needed to power through the tough or boring task in front of you.

Look on the bright side
A generally upbeat and optimistic outlook on life will keep your energy level up. Yes, the worst thing that can happen might actually happen, but giving it too much worry will only drain you. Look for the positive in every situation and you won't be so tired.

Get on your toes
Roll up and down on your toes. This stimulates your circulatory system, which will deliver much-needed oxygen and fuel (glucose) throughout your body. You'll be more energized and sharper. You can do this right now.

Listen to tunes while you work
It's well known that our brain's pleasure centers light up when we hear music. Throwing on headphones and listening to the music you like while working will give you a productivity boost.

Purge low-value tasks from your to-do list
If you have a ridiculously long to-do list that is impossible to get all the way through, you'll feel tired just thinking about it. If you want to actually cross off tasks from your list, you'll need to throw out the low-value tasks that you don't want/need to deal with. Either delegate these tasks, move them into a second "nice but not critical" list, or just admit that they're probably never going to get done and

move them to the "maybe/someday" list. Shortening your to-do list to just the most critical, must-do tasks will give you the energy to start knocking out those tasks.

Take a walk outside
Getting outside for some fresh air, a change of scenery, and a quick walk to get your blood flowing will do wonders for your mood and motivation. Seeing the sun is a signal to your body that it's not bedtime yet.

Socialize
Turn off the Internet and go socialize with friends. Humans are social animals, and we need regular socializing to keep ourselves in peak health and energy.

Take a weekend trip with a good friend or two
Go camping, wine tasting, or to wherever the road might take you. Pause your routine and stop to think about whatever is grinding you down. This will help you reconnect with fun, laughter, and adventure. There is nothing like new, exciting stories to help reenergize us.

READY, SET . . . OWN YOUR SH*T!

This adventure we call life often feels like an amusement-park ride we've ridden one too many times and now want off of. We get so dizzy we can't walk, think, or see straight. We become filled with regret and uncertainty and wish that we had stopped sooner when we saw the initial warning signs of uneasiness. We are now left to figure out how to stabilize ourselves and make the spinning stop.

But what are you going to do after the spinning stops? Are you going to get back on the ride only to suffer the same futile effects again? Or are you going to figure out how to learn from them and start moving forward to another ride or experience that you enjoy more?

Much of life is learned through trial and error. You don't create results by reading something from a book or website; results only come from acting on what you know and creating a visceral experience that you can learn upon next time. Much like the amusement-park ride, we tend to learn things in life by going out and making a bunch of decisions—mainly bad decisions in retrospect. You will eventually reach a point, however, where you get tired of both the bad decisions and the results that come from them. Inevitably it becomes pretty hard to keep making bad decisions over and over again without making a few good ones along the way.

It is through these good, bad, and indifferent decisions that you will become clear about both what you want and don't want in life. When you're frustrated and exhausted, you will finally be ready to try anything better to make the spinning end. You will stop trying to outthink life, and go with your natural flow.

We've explored a lot of ideas, tools, and techniques to gain greater understanding and to create big changes. Hopefully by now you have subjected yourself to the rigors of the Four Stages, but if you have skipped them or are still working through them but feel you're losing momentum or getting overwhelmed, remember this: My rule in life for "doing" is that if the task is not simple to comprehend, I won't do it. That doesn't mean it needs to be easy—just simple.

Here's what I mean: Up until a few years ago, I was a far less settled person. I was constantly juggling multiple jobs, phones, and to-do lists throughout the day. I was proud that I had dozens of things on the go, and I wore it like a badge of honor. But the more I tried to do, the less I got done, and the more frustrated I became. I was making micro progress on lots of things, but not building much momentum or results at any of them. I was spinning and getting dizzy and frustrated that the things I wanted were not showing up.

Eventually, I stopped trying to power my way through life and instead focused on one idea or task at a time—which is the essence of simplicity. When you're on an amusement-park ride, you only get dizzy when you have a scattered focus. If you pick a single point and stay focused on that point no matter where the ride takes you, when the ride stops you will have held your bearing and will not be dizzy. You will walk off the ride focused and ready for what's next.

I took this approach in my life. I stopped reading books on Internet marketing or how to build a $100,000-a-year business in six months and trying to do all the things they suggested. Instead,

I took single pieces of wisdom and tried to implement them in my life one change at a time. I also used this approach in my day-to-day multitasking. I no longer answered calls during meetings, responded to emails all hours of the day, or tried to talk with friends while out running. I let go of the worry and what-if and "should" that had plagued me in the past and focused on living a life of quality and not quantity.

Something amazing happened: I was able to make much greater progress on each task and got far better results and connection from it. I was doing less in each moment and yet gaining so much more value from it. My stress levels dropped because I worried less about what I had done or needed to do and instead paid attention to what I was doing in the moment. I went back to baby steps—one small thing at a time, moment after moment.

Using the Four Stages, pick something small in your life and start with that. Focus on the awareness of what's occurring there, what's missing, what you want for that area, and what small things you can do to make progress. I am sure you want to pick an area like your career, health, or relationship, but I suggest you start with the area of hobbies or what you do for fun. I bet you're not having a lot of fun anymore and thus not doing the things that make you feel like you. These are the creative outlets like writing, painting, playing your favorite sport, learning guitar, baking, gardening, or reading books by your favorite author. When we get frustrated, these are the first areas to go. We struggle to make progress on the bigger problems and don't allow ourselves to have any fun at anything else. Life becomes heavy when we lose touch with the small pleasures that make it worthwhile.

The only way to come up with new ideas or solutions for these bigger problems is to start having fun again. Joy, happiness, and creativity are the window into solving many of life's problems. You need to have these enjoyable moments in your day so you can build momentum that makes you feel like you again. Start small with smiling more; it's amazing how moving the sides of your mouth closer to your ears can change your entire life.